T.L. OSBORN

THE BEST of LIFE

SEVEN ENERGIZING TRUTHS

BOOKS BY THE OSBORNS

BELIEVERS IN ACTION—*Apostolic-Rejuvenating*
BIBLICAL HEALING—*Seven Miracle-Keys*
4 Visions–50+ yrs. of Proof–324 Merged Bible Vs.
FIVE CHOICES FOR WOMEN WHO WIN
21st Century Options
GOD'S BIG PICTURE—*An Impelling Gospel Classic*
GOD'S LOVE PLAN—*The Awesome Discovery*
HEALING THE SICK—*A Living Classic*
HOW TO BE BORN AGAIN—*The Miracle-Book*
JESUS ᴀɴᴅ WOMEN—*Big Questions Answered*
LIFE—TRAUMA AND TRIUMPH
A True Story of Life After Death
NEW LIFE FOR WOMEN—*Reality Refocused*
SOULWINNING–OUTSIDE THE SANCTUARY
A Classic on Biblical Christianity & Human Dignity
THE BEST OF LIFE—*Seven Energizing Dynamics*
THE GOOD LIFE—*A Mini-Bible School–1,467 Ref.*
THE GOSPEL ACCORDING TO T.L. & DAISY
Their Life & World Ministry–510 pg. Pictorial
THE MESSAGE THAT WORKS
T.L.'s Revealing Manifesto on Biblical Faith
THE POWER OF POSITIVE DESIRE
A Fresh Faith Perspective
STRATEGIC REFOCUS
Prayer—Demons—Spiritual Warfare
THE WOMAN BELIEVER
Awareness of God's Design
WOMAN WITHOUT LIMITS
Unmuzzled—Unfettered—Unimpeded
WOMEN & SELF-ESTEEM
Divine Royalty Unrestrained
YOU ARE GOD'S BEST
Transforming Life-Discoveries

OSBORN
PUBLISHERS

USA HQ:
OSBORN INTERNATIONAL
P.O. Box 10, Tulsa, OK 74102 USA

T.L. OSBORN, FOUNDER & PRES.
LADONNA OSBORN, VICE-PRES. & CEO

Tel: 918/743-6231
Fax: 918/749-0339   E-Mail: OSFO@aol.com
www.OSBORN.ORG

Canada: Box 281, Adelaide St. Post Sta., Toronto M5C 2J4
England: Box 148, Birmingham B3 2LG
(A Registered Charity)

> BIBLE QUOTATIONS IN THIS BOOK MAY BE PERSONALIZED, PARAPHRASED, ABRIDGED OR CONFORMED TO THE *PERSON* AND *TENSE* OF THEIR CONTEXTUAL APPLICATION IN ORDER TO FOSTER CLARITY AND INDIVIDUAL ACCEPTANCE. VARIOUS LANGUAGE TRANSLATIONS AND VERSIONS HAVE BEEN CONSIDERED. CHAPTER AND VERSE REFERENCES ENABLE THE READER TO COMPARE EACH BIBLICAL PASSAGE WITH HIS OR HER OWN BIBLE.
>
> THE AUTHOR

ISBN 0-87943-122-9
Copyright 2003 by LaDonna C. Osborn
Printed in the United States of America
All Rights Reserved

Contents

About the Author	9
Introduction	11

Section One—The Principle of SELF-VALUE
The Terrific "You" God Made

Part 1. You Are God's Best	17
Part 2. Everybody Is a Real Somebody	19
Part 3. The Best Possible You	22
Part 4. Seeds of Greatness Are in You	25
Part 5. You Are God's Starting Point	28
Part 6. Recognize Your Roots	31
Part 7. Welcome the Friendly Voice	34
60 Second Secret—Day One	39

Section Two—The Principle of IDENTITY
Your Key To Life's Best

Part 1. Your Link with God	43
Part 2. Two-Way Friendship	46
Part 3. Love's Idea	49
Part 4. You and God Can Come Home	53
Part 5. Good Things Happen	57
Part 6. The Way to Life's Best	59
Part 7. Saying "Thanks!" for Happiness	67
60 Second Secret—Day Two	69

Section Three—The Principle of DESIRE
Good Things Are for You

Part 1. Dream and Drive for It	73
Part 2. No Limit to Your Source	75
Part 3. It Is Right to Desire the Best	78
Part 4. The Good Life Is God's Idea	83
Part 5. Walk Tall—Success Is for NOW	87
Part 6. Help Yourself to God's Lifestyle	93
Part 7. Nothing Is Too Good for You	98
60 Second Secret—Day Three	103

Section Four—The Principle of DECISION
Your Power Secret

Part 1. You Are In Control	107

Part 2. You Are Deciding for Yourself ... 110
Part 3. How Much Is Enough for You ... 113
Part 4. A Beggar Can Become a Master ... 117
Part 5. You Are a Branch of God ... 119
Part 6. You and God Win Together ... 124
Part 7. God Depends on You ... 127
    60 Second Secret—Day Four ... 131

Section Five—The Principle of WEALTH
Your Big Connection

Part 1. There Is Plenty for You ... 143
Part 2. You Are Tapped into God's Wealth ... 147
Part 3. See Yourself in God's Class ... 151
Part 4. The High Purpose of Material Plenty ... 156
Part 5. God Has Big Ideas for You ... 160
Part 6. You Are Seeded for Abundance ... 166
Part 7. God's Generosity ... 170
    60 Second Secret—Day Five ... 181

Section Six—The Principle of VISION
Review the New *"You"*

Part 1. The *"YOU"* You See Is the *"YOU"* You'll Be ... 185
Part 2. Beyond Humanism to Unlimited Miracles ... 191
Part 3. Lifted to Dignity and Self Esteem ... 196
Part 4. Forming a New Image of Life ... 200
Part 5. Miracles Are Waiting in You ... 203
Part 6. Seeing Life's Best at Your House ... 208
Part 7. Now I See a Brand New Me ... 214
    60 Second Secret—Day Six ... 223

Section Seven—The Principle of ACTION
The Proof Of Your Faith

Part 1. The Great Awakener of Excellence ... 227
Part 2. Acting on the "Yes!" in Life ... 234
Part 3. Releasing God's Creative Power ... 240
Part 4. Start—and You Will Go Places ... 246
Part 5. Expand—S-t-r-e-t-c-h Yourself ... 250
Part 6. Energized with Enthusiasm ... 256
Part 7. Life Is a Glory—Not a Grind ... 260
    60 Second Secret—Day Seven ... 265
    OSBORN INTERNATIONAL Ministry To Millions ... 266

DEDICATED

To THOSE WHO want to make life beautiful and meaningful **now**;
To those who welcome each new day as a new adventure;
To those who chose
The BEST of LIFE.

T.L. Osborn

About The Author

IN THE MIDST of worldwide psychosocial fragmentation, Doctor T.L. Osborn's life and writings have expressed that which all of the philosophies and psychologies of people could not. This book with its powerful, profound, yet simply stated message is a distillation of nearly 60 years of sharing with millions in the developing and developed societies of the world. For nearly six decades, his audiences have numbered from 20,000 to over 250,000 in almost 90 nations.

This man and his wife, Daisy (deceased in 1995), have dealt face to face with people of practically every major religion and culture of our world.

Doctor Osborn does not claim to be a scholar of philosophy or psychology. He has learned what he shares from putting these principles to the test in people relationships.

He says, "Ideas are only useful when they benefit people and meet human needs: they must provide solutions and be workable in real life issues."

Whether teaching through the medium of an interpreter or speaking directly in French, Spanish or English, T. L. Osborn's expertise in communicating life's happiness and success secrets has been effective internationally. It has brought new meaning and understanding to those who doubted, and it has added fresh faith to those who were already believers.

His exposure to the kaleidoscope of human cultures and his diplomacy in sharing life's principles with varied and ofttimes sensitive and even reactionary audiences has developed in Dr. Osborn an unusual capacity for understanding people and a remarkable talent for motivating them to get life's best.

His credentials as a lifter of human persons are enhanced by his loyalty to common sense and practicality.

Doctor Osborn's sensitivity and perception of human emotions and needs are evident in his writings and recordings, and distinguish him from both philosophers and sermonizers.

The principles he shares are not derived from what he has read, but from applying them in the vast experiences he has lived.

—Carl R. Peterson, M.D., M.P.H.

INTRODUCTION

What You Can Get Out Of This Book

I HAVE WRITTEN THIS BOOK to show you how simply, quickly and easily you can get what you want out of life.

There are just a few basic secrets to discover.

They are within your reach.

No special education is necessary.

With these seven secrets — or principles, you can achieve your highest goals.

- You can get out of debt and off of welfare or social aid.
- You can acquire material success and personal fulfillment.
- You can win over inferiority and mediocrity.
- You can become a problem solver.
- You can surmount poverty and enjoy the good life.
- You can start over right where you are, and discover abilities in you that you never dreamed were there.
- You can enjoy a super-lifestyle with dignity and self-esteem.

- You can hook up to a dynamic energy that will make you a constant winner.
- You can possess anything you truly desire in life.
- You can break any destructive habit.
- You can discover the surest connection for prosperity, happiness and longevity.
- You can use the master key to life's BEST and open the wide gates to prosperity and fulfillment.
- You can experience *The BEST of LIFE.*

FOR FIFTY FOUR YEARS Daisy, my wife (deceased in 1995) and I enjoyed constant success, vibrant health, harmony and fulfillment in marriage, dynamic energy, superb happiness, true love — real living at its BEST.

God inspired and directed us in helping other people learn how to get life's BEST, too. The principles we always lived by and shared have worked like miracles **around the world,** wherever we journeyed together in crusades and seminars.

We discovered seven secrets in life. They produce a terrific lifestyle for anyone who practices them — and they are simple and easy to learn. Whether you are very young, an adult, middle-aged, or advanced in years, you can benefit rapidly.

INTRODUCTION

I have distilled the essence of each principle into a *60-second secret*. This way, you can master them all, 60 seconds at a time, in just seven days.

These seven principles have been tested and proven in the arena of human experience all over the world.

We have presented them in face to face teaching sessions among Buddhists, Moslems, Shintoists, Hindus, animists, fetish worshippers, Christians and atheists—to people of most of the major cultures and religions of our world.

This book is my way of sharing these proven principles with YOU if you *want* to live and prosper, in health and happiness, and experience life's BEST.

- Heads of State, Governors, Commissioners and Mayors have welcomed us to teach these secrets and to lift their people.
- Politicians have realized new human-value and have risen to greater success and esteem in their areas.
- People who were actually beggars have been lifted from self-repudiation to new purpose and achievement—some now own their own businesses.
- Women have discovered new values and have climbed out of traditional mediocrity on to new levels of growth and achievement.
- University students of both sexes have applied these seven secrets and have attained success in business and leadership.

THE BEST OF LIFE

- Multiplied thousands have learned and embraced these principles and have been raised from poverty to good living, from sickness to health, from fear to confidence, from shame to self-esteem.
- Poor people have accepted and acted on these principles and are now experiencing the good life.
- Incurable sicknesses have been miraculously healed.
- Broken families have been restored and are now enjoying tranquility and happiness.
- Used and abused people have attained self-respect, self-value and self-esteem.
- Alcohol, tobacco and chemical dependents have been totally and miraculously rehabilitated.
- Loneliness and fear have disappeared in the glow of new faith and vital purpose in life.

All of this will now begin to work for *you!*

You are marked for the BEST in life. This book in your hands signals a new beginning for you. It could be God's way of saying: *"I love you! I want to help you! You have great worth. You are too valuable to ever be a loser! I'll be with you! Nothing will be impossible for you and me!"*

So, learn these secrets and determine to experience **The BEST of LIFE**.

—T.L. Osborn

SECTION ONE

THE PRINCIPLE OF SELF-VALUE

THE TERRIFIC "YOU" GOD MADE

SECTION 1

Part 1 — You Are God's Best	17
Part 2 — Everybody Is a Real Somebody	19
Part 3 — The Best Possible You	22
Part 4 — Seeds of Greatness Are in You	25
Part 5 — You Are God's Starting Point	28
Part 6 — Recognize Your Roots	31
Part 7 — Welcome the Friendly Voice	34
60 Second Secret — Day One	39

SECTION 1—Part 1

You Are God's Best

THE FIRST SECRET I will share with you is easy to learn, yet so powerful that it will actually start the miracle you need in life while you are reading this book.

You will look at what was an impossibility and say, *"Now I know what to do, what to say, how to deal with this and win!"*

Destiny is now at work in *you*.

Why were you chosen for this information which has lifted tens of thousands of people around the world?

It is God's way of saying:

> "I love you. I created my BEST when I created you. I paid a price for you and you are worth all I ever paid for you! I have predestined my BEST for you!"

When I give you this first secret, be like Thomas Edison. Someone asked him how he gave the world so many inventions. He said: "Because I never think in *words*, I think in *pictures.*"

So...let your mind soar.

> ## SECRET NUMBER ONE
>
> YOU ARE CREATED in the image of God, to be like Him, to manifest him in human form. You are made for *life* and *love*—for *power* and *prosperity*—for *success* and *dignity*.

God made nothing inferior. He is first class all the way. He created you unique. You are exceptional—one-of-a-kind.

Before you were born, you existed in God's mind. He knew this world would need you at this time. He planned you with a special purpose that no one but **you** could fulfill **because no one on earth could** do what you are here to do.

SECTION 1—Part 2

Everybody Is a Real Somebody

An INSANE MAN was brought to one of our teaching meetings overseas. Fifty thousand people were there.

He was known as the running maniac. His hair and beard were long, disheveled and flea-infested. His body was filthy. His rags barely covered his nakedness.

God never created anybody to be unable to think and act normally, or to live in shame and disgrace.

I did not know that the insane man was in the audience as I planted the seeds of HUMAN VALUE in the minds of the people.

There is a miraculous power in truth. I believe words are seeds. They have ability to produce what they say. They are energizers.

I told that audience:

"Each one of you is beautifully and wonderfully made—in God's image. Every individual among you is special. You do not have to be second class. You are each unique. God who created you like Himself, put you here for a purpose so special that no one else on earth can do what you are here to do."

Those *word-seeds* had power.

There is a remarkable statement in the Bible about the power of Jesus' words.

As He was teaching, the power of the Lord was there to heal the people.^{Lu.5:17}

That has to be what happened to the insane man who was brought to our meeting that day.

We taught that crowd the essence of what I will share with you in this book. We emphasized that God made no one for failure, poverty, sickness or shame; **that *everybody* is a real *somebody* in God's eyes.**

I urged that audience to personally accept the fact that each of them was a special creation of God and to begin believing that by cooperating with God, any person could realize the BEST in life.

In some miraculous way those seeds of truth penetrated that insane man and his mind was healed and his life was transformed.

Before those teaching sessions were over, that man was perfectly normal. He was clean, groomed and wearing a suit. He attended every meeting, listening, learning and developing into a remarkably balanced gentleman.

The power of the truths I will share in this book, brought him all the way from a running, half-naked, wild man to a groomed, well dressed gentleman. He found good employment and has become a positive influence in his community. He is a living example of one who rose from emptiness to meaningful living.

No human being was ever created to be inferior. God never planned for anyone to be lonely, defeated, unhealthy, destructive or despondent.

God created YOU in His own image, to live His life, to walk and to talk with Him, to think, plan and act with Him.

SECTION 1—Part 3

The Best Possible You

CREATED IN GOD'S image, you are his kind of being!

Accept your *self-value*. See the picture of yourself as God's masterpiece—regardless of your present state of affairs.

An artist was attracted by a beggar who sat across the pathway. Thinking of God's handiwork in every human being, the perceptive artist painted the man as he imagined him to potentially become. Then he called the beggar to see the painting.

"Is that me?" the beggar asked.

"That is the you I see in you!" replied the artist.

"If that's the man you see in me," the beggar stated with new purpose in his eyes, "then that's the man I shall be!"

The seeds of greatness are in you. By accepting this first principle, you are causing those seeds to begin growing in you right now while you read.

THE BEST POSSIBLE YOU

Your God-given value does not depend on special genes from superior parents. Your worth before God is not measured by your assets, the color of your skin, super intelligence or formal education.

Created by God, you are a part of God.

It is right that you esteem what God esteems and value what God values.

All sorts of miracles start happening when you discover and accept your value and your potential.

The Bible says, *You are God's workmanship.*^{Eph. 2:10} [Eph. 2:10]

The man who wrote most of the Psalms was wonder-struck by how God made human persons.

You have made people a little less than God, [King James Version— *"angels;"* Original Hebrew, French and certain other language-versions— *"God."*] *and You crown them with glory and honor. You have given them dominion over the works of Your hands; You have put all things under their feet.*^{Psa.8:5-6} [Psa. 8:5-6]

The bottom line of positive and stable self-esteem is when you can say:

"I accept the value that God has put on me."

When you do that, you will then cooperate with God to develop the BEST possible *you* in this world.

THE BEST OF LIFE

Self-Value will rid you of all jealousy because you will never again want to be anyone else.

Self-Value will wipe out inferiority because you are in God's class of being and *He, in you, is greater than any person or any power outside of you.* 1Jn.4:4

Self-Value will eliminate fear of failure or defeat because nothing can stop you and God working together.

Self-Value will give you courage because you discover that with God at work in you, you become indomitable.

Self-Value will cause you to stand up tall, to square your shoulders, to look out into the future with new confidence, to walk with a steady stride, and to rise to the level of the importance for which God created you.

SECTION I—Part 4

Seeds of Greatness Are in You

IN GENESIS 1:27 the Bible says:

So God created people in his own image. [Then it is repeated.] ***In the image of God created He him; male and female created He them.***

Genesis 5:1 adds that you were created *in the likeness of God.*

God created human persons as much like Himself as any child can be like its natural parents.

Later the Bible informs us that Adam and Eve bore a son, Seth.

The same words are used to describe Seth's resemblance to Adam, his father, as are used to describe your resemblance to God, your Father.

Adam…begat a son *in his own likeness, after his own image.*[Gen.5:3]

You see, whatever one can say about parents can be said of their offspring.

THE BEST OF LIFE

God planned that whatever could be said about HIM, could be said about YOU.

The Bible explains the lifestyle and plan God designed for you and me.

God said, Be fruitful and multiply, and replenish the earth, and subdue it: and have dominion over every living thing.^{Gen.1:28}

In verses 29-30, all of the possessions on earth that God gave to humankind are listed.

God never planned you or me for poverty, inferiority, sickness, depression, want or insecurity.

God never created anything inferior — not you — not any human person.

As this powerful principle takes root, you begin to see and respect yourself as a member of Divine Royalty.

God's family is supposed to represent Him and to reflect His lifestyle on earth.

You ask, "What can I do about it?"

The seven secrets I shall share in this book will show you.

The first step is to recognize your value. When you do, you cause the seeds of greatness to germinate in you.

SEEDS OF GREATNESS ARE IN YOU

Keep those seeds watered by thinking on them and reaffirming your value until your attitude and conduct are transformed.

Those seeds will grow. It will be like a miracle at work in you.

You begin to think and feel and talk like someone of value and of dignity.

Your self-value commands respect.

Others treat you like you treat yourself.

They see you like you see yourself.

You merit the confidence of others when you practice trusting yourself.

You stamp your own value on your life by your very own thoughts, words and actions.

Never entertain demeaning thoughts about yourself again. Never speak or act as a second class person.

SECTION I—Part 5

You Are God's Starting Point

KEEP THE PICTURE of God's kind of being in your mind. Self-value and self-esteem are the noblest garments you can wear.

Purpose to never discredit the you that God values so much.

Determine to never demean the you that God created in His own image.

Once you accept your own value with God, you will be able to value others.

As you care about yourself, you will care about others.

Everything from God is channeled through you. The stronger God can be in you, the more He can lift others through you.

The more love that fills you, the more love you will discover being expressed through you.

Poor people cannot help poor people.

YOU ARE GOD'S STARTING POINT

Down people cannot lift down people.

Only happy people can make others happy.

Only positive people can make others positive.

You are God's starting point.

The greatest possible achievement in life is to *be* the terrific person God created you to *be*.

To disregard that noble purpose results in frustration, unhappiness and deterioration.

The reason there is so much loneliness, depression, drug and sex abuse, insecurity and even suicide, is because people do not value themselves.

They see themselves as a speck in the universe, a number in a computer, of no personal significance. They look into their mirror and feel insignificant, helpless and hopeless.

But when you discover your value as a creation of God, to represent Him, your life takes on purpose, a reason for being. You suddenly realize:

> I am made for success. I was not put here to stand in a social-aid line, to feel shame nor to be lonely.
>
> God and I can walk together. We can change our world.

You look in the mirror as a new day dawns, and you no longer see a despondent, rejected and downcast *nobody*. You see God's *creation in human flesh*.

THE BEST OF LIFE

You say:

> Good morning, God. I see your handiwork in me. I am masterfully made—created to be Your partner.
>
> God, You look great in me this morning. What good and productive things are You and me up to today?

To succeed with purpose and to get life's BEST, the first principle is to recognize your *Self-Value.*

Understand your potential.

You are like Columbus gazing at the new world he had discovered. There are valuable treasures to be uncovered and developed. They will turn you into a successful, happy, healthy, and productive achiever, and countless others will share in the benefits.

Your thinking is like electricity that can be captured, harnessed and channeled into creative productivity for YOURSELF and for the good of others.

The most powerful concept you can hold is that God is in you. Your life is the very breath of God.

God's life in you—means His LOVE is in you, limitless, healing, lifting, blessing you—**and others through you.**

SECTION I—Part 6

Recognize Your Roots

GOD'S LIFE IN YOU means that His power is there in YOU, immeasurable, miraculous, positive, productive—and flowing out to others through YOU.

You need never feel abandoned or alone, guilty or condemned.

You need never feel inferior or without value, confused or without purpose, afraid or anxious.

When you recognize your roots in God and see yourself as His intended habitation; when you discover how easy it is to experience God in you, you will actually have a rebirth of Self-Worth.

Your very life becomes the miracle of God's *Life* breathed into you.

People begin to respect you and to draw strength and inspiration from you. This is because you have discovered self-respect, self-value and self-esteem which is the basis for a positive and enthusiastic outlook on life.

You begin to count on God inside of you because you allow Him to live within you.

You begin to think and talk like those who trusted God in Bible days.

I have paraphrased for you some of the powerful statements in Psalm 91:

> God is your refuge and strength. He delivers you from every snare and pestilence.
>
> He covers you. His truth is your armor. You are not afraid, day or night. Though tragedy strikes all around you, your security is in God. Nothing destroys Him and He lives in you.
>
> No evil befalls you. No plague comes to your dwelling because God is there. His angels keep charge over you wherever you go. They even bear you up above any danger that is in your way.
>
> You are able to walk right over any enemy that intends to injure or destroy you.
>
> These blessings are because God has set His love upon you and you have set your love upon Him. He knows your name and sets you in a high place.
>
> When you call upon Him, He answers you. He is with you in trouble. He delivers you and honors you. He satisfies you with long life and shows you His salvation.

RECOGNIZE YOUR ROOTS

The human person is the only creature on this earth that yearns for self-respect, self-value and self-esteem.

People cannot tolerate life without dignity. They will withdraw into rooms and close the blinds. They will become recluses from society, or lay down in ditches or gutters and gradually die, the victims of lonely and purposeless abandonment.

The reason I am writing this book for you is to show you the way and to encourage you to resolve to experience *The BEST of LIFE!*

The curse of resignation, the cancer of futility and abandonment only develop in people who fail to discover their **self-value, their dignity and their potential for happy prosperous living.**

SECTION 1–Part 7

Welcome the Friendly Voice

For THOUSANDS of years, the way to God's BEST in life has been defined clearly in the Bible, but human-beings do not always accept those beautiful ideas because of religious prejudice.

The barrage of conflicting religious doctrines frighten people away from God.

Humanism has tried for centuries to make a more attractive appeal based on logistics and reason. Seeking to placate the conscience of people, they cry: "Humankind is *good!*"

Traditional religious orators say, "No! We must stress the basic fact that humankind is *bad!*"

Both arguments miss the point because they focus attention upon the human person in itself.

Rather than to argue either that "People are *bad*" or that "People are *good*," the positive option transcends all human assessment and builds on the foundation that "*God is good!*"

WELCOME THE FRIENDLY VOICE

If God is good, YOU can be good. Since He created you in His own image and likeness, YOU can have dignity and *Self-Value*.

One can never exalt God by demeaning His offspring.

I have been criticized because I do not stand before audiences and expose or assail or condemn the sins of people.

A human person who has not found the way to God, is already conscious of guilt and condemnation.

I choose to point you to God who is *good*. He loves you in whatever state you may be, so much that He paid the supreme price of giving His own Son, Jesus, to redeem you from all sin by suffering the penalty for your sin, *in your place*—and He did it before you ever knew you needed it.

Since He loved you that much—even when you were oblivious to His goodness, that gives you reason to believe that you have *divine value and dignity*.

Whether you are basically *good* (as the humanists and psychologists say), or *bad* (as the priests, rabbis and preachers say) really doesn't matter. Without God, you are not normal. You are not living up to your potential.

THE BEST OF LIFE

So welcome the *friendly voice* that does not attack and condemn you, but that honestly gives you hope by reminding you that God is there, powerful, loving and caring.

Welcome the *friendly message* of the gospel that tells you that God created you to be exactly like Him; that your purpose is to be Him in action; that He so valued you that He paid an infinite price to redeem you from inferiority, deterioration and sin.

Once you understand this and accept it, God can share His life in and through you.

You may be overwhelmed by this information. You may have thought you were a *nobody*.

But God's *friendly voice* encourages you to look beyond your humanity to His *Love*. Keep in focus the fact that all of the time that you were in shame, God kept right on loving you. He created you so that He could live in you.

Perhaps you never heard anyone tell you that you are like God.

Your conscience condemns you. Sermonizers threaten and frighten you. Your own habits and life-style undermine you. You may be alone, afraid and guilty.

Now this *friendly voice* lifts you by reminding you of your origin in God, of your design for suc-

WELCOME THE FRIENDLY VOICE

cess. Your purpose is to be an achiever. You are God's creation.

Look beyond yourself, and see God. Begin to sense dignity and self-value. Let your heart leap with new hope. Say:

I want to let God in. I am created for greatness. I respond to this *friendly, gentle voice* that brings me *good* News. This is what I am made for. This is the way to the BEST in life!

I am not worthless. God thinks I am worth everything He paid to redeem me. He gives me dignity and self-esteem because He created me!

Now I have discovered my value, who I really am, what I am really for.

I am thankful. I am somebody. I understand now, why it was necessary for me to discover the principle of my *Self-Value.*

THE BEST OF LIFE

WELCOME THE FRIENDLY VOICE

60 SECOND SECRET

DAY ONE

I AM VALUABLE because I am created in God's class of being.

I am *vital* because God's plan involves me.

My *heritage* is to have God's best, to enjoy His companionship and to use His wealth and power for the good of myself and others.

I am created for life, love, power, prosperity, success and dignity.

The seeds of greatness are in me. God never created me to be a **"Nobody"**, but a real **"Somebody"**.

I therefore recognize my *Self-Value*, that God designed me for His lifestyle and I now know that He planned life's BEST for me as His child.

I shall no longer discredit or demean or destroy what God created in His own image and values so much.

I welcome **God's** *friendly voice.* He reminds me of my divine origin, of my high purpose, and of His Love Plan to help me achieve, enjoy and share His BEST in life.

THE BEST OF LIFE

SECTION TWO

THE PRINCIPLE OF IDENTITY

YOUR KEY TO LIFE'S BEST

SECTION 2

Part 1 — Your Link with God	43
Part 2 — Two-Way Friendship	46
Part 3 — Love's Idea	49
Part 4 — You and God Can Come Home	53
Part 5 — Good Things Happen	57
Part 6 — The Way to Life's Best	59
Part 7 — Saying "Thanks!" for Happiness	67
60 Second Secret — Day Two	69

SECTION 2—Part I

Your Link with God

NOW YOU HAVE discovered your value.

God Himself proved how much He esteems you by the price He paid for you—the price of His Son. *Christ died for our sins...*^{1Cor.15:3} His act of love ends all argument about your worth.

Realizing this, you are ready for the most powerful and dynamic experience a human being can have.

You are ready to *Identify* with this God in a personal encounter.

This second principle that I call *IDENTITY* is the most powerful key in this entire book because it is the one that opens the gates to God's riches, health, success and blessings. That is why I call it, Your key to Life's Best.

> ## SECRET NUMBER TWO
>
> *Understand WHO Jesus Christ is, WHY He came, WHY He was put to death, WHY He came back from the dead and HOW He lives today.* Then *Identify* with Him in a personal way because *He is your link with God and success.*

To understand *why* Jesus Christ came and *how* to *identify* with Him, you need to understand the problem that existed in the human race at the beginning.

God's dream for humanity is recorded in the Bible book of Genesis. His plan was to reproduce **Himself** in Adam and Eve and to have companionship with them.

Adam and Eve were not required or forced to respect God any more than you are.

God placed them in the Garden of Eden and gave them *every tree that is pleasant to the eye and good for food; and the tree of life also in the midst of the garden.*^{Gen.2:9}

God made one single restriction to measure their faith and confidence in His dream for them. He said:

*You may eat from every tree in the garden except the tree of knowing good and evil...the day you eat from it **you will certainly die**.*^{Gen.2:16-17}

YOUR LINK WITH GOD

They were expected to have confidence in what God said and that is all that He expects of you and of me.

If Adam and Eve trusted in God's integrity, they would live and prosper with Him forever. If they abused His trust and disbelieved His word, the process of deterioration would begin and they would die.

Their lack of trust in the integrity of what God said was later called *"Sin."*

The simple rule that God made was: *The person who sins will **die**.*[Eze.18:4,20]

Later it was repeated in another way: *The wages of sin is **death**.*[Rom.6:23]

SECTION 2—Part 2

Two-Way Friendship

GOD WANTED THE human persons whom He had created to have total happiness, divine purpose and abundant living.

But their friendship had to be two-way. God would need to be sure that Adam and Eve wanted Him, like He wanted them.

What actually transpired shows us what sin really is.

Satan, God's enemy, heard of God's dream and conceived a scheme to induce Adam and Eve to betray God's trust.

Satan came into the garden and spoke with Eve, urging her to eat of the forbidden tree. He contradicted God, asserting himself as an authority and said:

If you eat of that tree, *you will NOT die.*^{Gen.3:4}

The woman was convinced. *So she ate of the fruit and gave some to her husband, and he ate too.*^{Gen.3:6}

TWO-WAY FRIENDSHIP

Result:

God came into the garden and, after questioning Adam and Eve, spelled out for them what the results would be:

There would be no grounds for a relationship with God. Adam and Eve had exercised their free wills and had, by their action, disregarded and disbelieved what God had said. The good life ended.

So, the integrity of God required the full measure of His law. Otherwise, His word could never be trusted.

Adam and Eve were no longer qualified to dwell in the Garden with God. Separated from His plenty and beyond His protection, they were now subject to their new "master."

That was the beginning of suffering, disease, pain, hate, lust, envy, murder, jealousy, loneliness, guilt, poverty, hunger, destruction and death.

Sin had entered the human race. It would be passed on to all generations.

Whereas, by one person sin entered into the world, and death by sin; so death passed upon all persons, for that all have sinned. Rom.5:12

The fundamental **sin** that severed God's relationship with humankind was not murder or adultery or lying or stealing or hatred or abuse.

It was the assumption or philosophy or attitude that *God did not mean what he said.*

When that position is taken, deterioration sets in like a cancer and is terminal.

When you do not trust God, you do not trust yourself — or anyone else.

When you decide that God has no integrity, your own integrity is abandoned. Conscience is calloused. Dignity is deprecated. The human person deteriorates and dies. The light goes out. There is only darkness.

Could that be society's problem today?

Without trust in God's integrity, human persons sink into despair and disgrace, degeneration and disease, destruction and oblivion.

SECTION 2—Part 3

Love's Idea

GOD NEVER ABANDONED His dream for you.

God is *Love* and *Love Never Quits*.

His love went into action the day Adam and Eve sinned. He found a just and legal way to restore humankind back to an intimate relationship with Him.

His love plan would end the scourge of death and restore people to *Life*.

What was His love plan and how could it restore you to God and legally absolve you from the penalty of death for your sins?

"Substitution" was the legal answer.

If someone who is innocent of sin would willingly take the place of one who is guilty and assume full punishment for his or her sins, then the guilty one would be free and could be restored to friendship with God as though no wrong had ever been done.

It was *Love's* idea.

Now you can understand why Jesus Christ came and died for you.

God so **loved** *the world that He gave His only begotten Son, that whoever believes in Him should not perish but have everlasting Life.*^{Jn.3:16}

In order to provide you a substitute who had no sin of his own, God gave **His own Son.**

Jesus was born by a miracle conception. The spirit of God overshadowed a virgin and the seed of divine life was created in her womb. In that way Jesus was not born of human seed that was infected by sin.

Not only **His conception, but His life among people** must be sinless, in order to be **your** *Substitute.*

God's Son must be subjected to the same temptations of sin as any human person is. He must be exactly like you and resist what human persons had not resisted. He must prove that God's original plan could work — that human persons could choose God's word, and never dishonor His integrity.

Jesus must be tempted by Satan just as Adam and Eve had been.

LOVE'S IDEA

This is why as soon as He was mature, Jesus was led into the wilderness where Satan came to tempt Him exactly as he had come to tempt Adam and Eve in the garden of Eden.

Every time Satan tried to bring question on God's Word, Jesus rejected his suggestions and forthrightly *asserted what God had said.*^{Mat.4:1-11}

Under the most trying circumstances, **Jesus believed God's Word.**

The Bible says that throughout the earthly life of Christ, He was *in every respect tested as we are, yet without committing any sin.*^{Heb.4:15}

Jesus Christ was perfect. He was untouched by the *seed* of sin.

That explains why He **was able to be your substitute. Since He had no sin in Him, and He committed no sin, He could assume your sins and give His life as a ransom for us.**

If **your** penalty of death was **assumed by Him, YOU would be legally absolved of the penalty.**

Since no debt can be paid twice, or no crime punished twice, you would be restored as though you had never done wrong.

Since Jesus Christ suffered the penalty you and I deserved, and since He did it on your behalf, YOU are no longer guilty before God and need never be judged for any sin that you have ever committed.

THE BEST OF LIFE

The judgment YOU deserved was put on your substitute, in your place, and that judgment can never be imposed on you again.

This is the crux of God's *Love* in the Bible that we call *Salvation*.

SECTION 2—Part 4

You and God Can Come Home

GOD'S LOVE PLAN for you, just like His original dream, is based on faith in His integrity—confidence and trust in His word. His only condition for you is that you simply honor and trust what He says.

The plan depends on your willingness to *identify* with the one who died as your substitute.

This is your key to *Life's BEST*.

This involves your *will*.

You have the right of choice. You are free to accept the validity of what Christ did on your behalf, or to reject it as superstition or irrelevant or insignificant.

God's love plan depends entirely on faith, just like He required Adam and Eve to trust His integrity.

Anyone who believes in Jesus Christ is not judged at all.[Jn.3:18]

THE BEST OF LIFE

All who trust God's Son to save them have eternal life.^{Jn.3:36}

What specifically are you to "trust" or "believe"?

1. That Jesus was sinless and perfect;
2. That He died on **your** behalf and bore the judgment you should bear;
3. That He did it because God loves you and wants to live with you;
4. That God values You so much that He paid this infinite price to make that possible.

These remarkable facts are what is called the *"Gospel"* or *good* News.

- He suffered the penalty of your sins so that you can be saved from death and live eternally as He planned for you.
- He suffered the consequences of your sins so that you can be forever absolved from guilt, condemnation or judgment.
- He took upon Himself your pains, infirmities and sicknesses, so that you can be free of them and live in health and enjoy longevity.
- He bore your insecurity, shame, inferiority and loneliness, so that you can live in fellowship with God again.
- He died so that you can live.
- He assumed your guilt so that you can receive His righteousness.

YOU AND GOD CAN COME HOME

God took the sinless Christ and poured into Him your sins. Then, in exchange, He pours God's goodness into you.^{2Cor.5:21LB}

The record of your sins was credited to Christ's account. Then He assumed your guilt and bore the judgment that you deserved.

In exchange, His righteousness was credited to your account and you were declared "righteous" in God's eyes, forever.

When does this happen?

When you decide to *Identify* with what Jesus Christ did, and when you believe that He assumed the judgment for your sins in your place. When you do that, you will experience a miracle.

The righteousness of Christ will be transferred to you and you will be free of all guilt and judgment.

Jesus Christ will come and live the life of God in and through you.

You will become a new creation.

You will be restored to God according to His original plan.

A supernatural power will be given to you which will make you a child of God. It will be a miracle.

This is your key to Life's BEST.

Christ opened the way for God to come to you and for you to come to Him. He is your link with

THE BEST OF LIFE

God, your way to THE GOOD LIFE. (Request my book that title which was written as a *Mini-Bible School* for new converts abroad. It has 1,467 Bible references.)

SECTION 2—Part 5

Good Things Happen

WHEN YOU WELCOME Jesus Christ into your life by faith, there are several miraculous results.

These results can take place in you today — now, because, *Now is the accepted time; Now is the day of salvation* — for YOU.[2Cor.6:2]

FIRST: *You are re-born,* re-created, restored to God and made new. You become a child of God.

When you receive Jesus Christ, God gives you the miracle *power to become His child.*[Jn.1:12]

SECOND: *You receive a new spiritual life,* the miracle life of God through Jesus Christ in you.

If you are in Christ, you are a new creature. All things become new.[2Cor.5:17]

Jesus said, *I am come that you might have Life more abundantly.*^{Jn.10:10}

THIRD: *You receive total peace.* Anxiety, hypertension, fear, guilt and condemnation are gone forever.

Jesus said, *Peace I leave with you, my peace I give unto you.*^{Jn.14:27}

Being justified by faith, you have peace with God through your Lord Jesus Christ.^{Rom.5:1}

FOURTH: *You are restored to friendship,* fellowship and life with God — the way you were designed to live on this earth.

Truly your fellowship is with the Father, and with his Son Jesus Christ.^{1Jn.1:3}

FIFTH: *Your physical body is affected* so much by this new inner peace with God that your sicknesses disappear and you experience new physical and mental health.

You will serve the Lord your God, and He will take sickness away from the midst of you.^{Ex.23:25}

The Lord *forgives all of your iniquities; He heals all of your diseases.*^{Psa.103:3}

SECTION 2—Part 6

The Way to Life's Best

BEFORE I GUIDE YOU in your act of faith to receive God's Life by accepting Jesus Christ, I will outline for you the way to be restored to God.

FIRST: Believe you are valuable, as God's creation.

For you are God's workmanship.^{Eph.2:10}

God created people in His own image,^{Gen.1:27} *in the likeness of God.*^{Gen.5:1-2}

The Lord has made people a little lower than God, [King James Version— "angels;" Original Hebrew, French and certain other language-versions— "God."] *and crowned them with glory and honor. The Lord gave them dominion over the works of his hands; He put all things under their feet.*^{Psa.8:5-6}

SECOND: Know that *distrusting God's Word* is the original and basic problem.

*And the Lord told Adam and Eve, Of every tree of the garden you may freely eat; but of the tree of the knowledge of good and evil, you will **not** eat of it; for in the day that you eat of it you will surely die.*^{Gen.2:16-17}

Satan influenced them to distrust God's word. He contradicted God by saying: *you will **not** surely die.*^{Gen.3:4}

*Eve took of the fruit and ate it, and gave some to her husband **with her;** and he ate it.*^{Gen.3:6}

That was the original sin—*distrusting God's Word.*

THIRD: Understand that disavowing God's integrity results in *death.*

God said, in the day that you disavow my instructions and eat the fruit I forbade, *you will surely die.*^{Gen.2:17}

The wages of sin [disavowing the integrity of God's Word] *is death.*^{Rom.6:23}

Whereas, by one person sin entered into the world, and death by sin; so death passed upon all persons, for that all have sinned.^{Rom.5:12}

THE WAY TO LIFE'S BEST

FOURTH: Believe that God valued you too much to let you die.

God was *not willing that **any** should perish, but that **all** should come to repentance.*^{2Pe.3:9}

*God so loved the world that He gave His only begotten Son, that **whoever** believes in Him will **not** perish, but have everlasting **Life**.*^{Jn.3:16}

*But God showed **His great love for you by sending Christ to die for you**.*^{Rom.5:8}

FIFTH: Know *why* Jesus came and died as your substitute.

Since the penalty of sin is death,^{Rom.6:23} and since *death passed upon all persons because **all** have sinned,*^{Rom.5:12} All would have to die for their sins — unless a guiltless substitute would willingly pay our penalty by dying in our place.

Jesus Christ, God's Son *was in all points tempted like as we are, yet without sin.*^{Heb.4:15} *He did no sin.*^{1Pe.2:22}

Being made perfect, Jesus Christ became the author of eternal salvation.^{Heb.5:9}

Jesus Christ bore our sins in His own body, that we, being dead to sins, should live unto righteousness.^{1Pe.2:24}

THE BEST OF LIFE

God made Jesus Christ who knew no sin to be made sin on our behalf, so that in Him we might share the righteousness [or Life] of God. 2Cor.5:21

SIXTH: Identify with Christ's death, burial and resurrection.

   1. When Jesus Christ *died,* your old life of sin died with Him. Identify with His death for you.

     I have been crucified with Christ. Gal.2:20

   2. When Jesus Christ was *buried,* your old life of sin was put away forever. Identify with His burial on your behalf.

     We are buried with Jesus Christ into death. Rom.6:4

   3. When Jesus Christ was *raised* from the dead, you were raised up with Him. Identify with His resurrection.

     God has raised Jesus Christ from the dead and has quickened you together with Him, having forgiven you all trespasses. Col.2:12-13

   4. **When Jesus Christ arose in a *New Life,*** you arose to walk in that same new life of God. Identify with the new *Life* of Christ.

     Like as Christ was raised up from the dead by the glory of the Father, even so we also should walk in NEWNESS OF LIFE. Rom.6:4

     You are risen with Christ. Col.3:1

     Christ is your life. Col.3:4

THE WAY TO LIFE'S BEST

SEVENTH: Believe the gospel and receive Jesus Christ in person now.

God's love plan is based on faith in the integrity of His word and on your right to choose to believe.

Believe on the Lord Jesus Christ and you will be saved.^{Ac.16:31}

As many as receive Jesus Christ, He gives to them power to become the children of God.^{Jn.1:12}

Identify with Jesus Christ because He is the way, the bridge, the link or the key that makes possible your reunion with God and God's reunion with you.

YOU can now come home to God who created you and values you.

GOD can now come home to you and live in and through you, which was His original dream.

Right now, find a place alone with God. Get on your knees and pray this prayer, out loud.

O GOD, my Father in heaven:

It was You, who wonderfully created me, in Your own image and likeness. My life has great value.

I know I must never destroy what You created. I must never depreciate what You value or despise what You love.

THE BEST OF LIFE

I now know that I am made to walk with You. I was never created for loneliness, sickness, inferiority or guilt.

By ignoring Your life and love, I have disregarded Your integrity and Your honor. This has separated me from Your life and goodness.

Without Your life, all that remains is deterioration and death.

O FATHER IN HEAVEN, *I see now that when You created me, Your dream was to live in me.*

You had such love for me that You found a way to save me from deterioration and death.

You gave Your Son, Jesus Christ to come to this world. He was tempted every way possible but He never sinned. He never distrusted Your word or denied Your integrity. He was perfect and without sin.

He became my substitute and assumed the punishment for all of my sins, when He died on the cross.

I do here and now, Identify with Jesus Christ.

When He died, my old sinful life died.

When Jesus was buried, my old sinful life was buried.

When Jesus was raised up from the dead in a new life, His new life was offered to me.

THE WAY TO LIFE'S BEST

You promised that if I received Jesus Christ by faith, Your power would recreate me as Your child and I would have the new Christ-Life.

I do, here and now, open my heart and receive Jesus Christ as my Savior and Lord, and I accept His new Life in me.

I believe that as I receive Jesus, I receive You, O God.

I do believe that You have now come back to live in me like You originally planned when You created me.

I believe I am saved. You and I are one again because of what Your Son, Jesus, did in my place.

O, JESUS, MY LORD, *since You paid the full price for my transgressions, there can never be any further price for me to pay.*

I believe that I am saved, here, now and forever because of the good news of what You accomplished when You died in my place.

Now I am restored to God my Father through Jesus my Savior.

DEAR FATHER, *all of the abundance You created on this earth is for my blessing. Now, You will supply everything I need, and guide me in obtaining it.*

You are my Great Physician. You know how wonderfully I am made. You live in me

THE BEST OF LIFE

now. Your miracle life is the healing life in me now.

There will be no more loneliness, O Lord, because You are my friend. You live in me and I in You.

My sins are punished. They can never be punished again. My debt is paid. No debt can ever be paid twice.

I am saved — here and now.

I believe, and I am free.

Thank You, O Father, and thank You Lord Jesus. Amen.

SECTION 2—Part 7

Saying "Thanks!" for Happiness

NOW YOU ARE restored to God, to honor, to dignity and to self-worth.

A miracle life has begun in you.

That is why I wrote this book.

Write to me and we will reply. We will be friends in helping other people discover *The Way* of restoration to God's lifestyle.

From the day your letter reaches us, we will be earnestly praying for God's BEST to come to you and to your loved ones.

We will send you a list of other books we have written to help you. One is titled, THE GOOD LIFE — over 300 pages of terrific, power-filled ideas to help you experience life's BEST.

We have recorded some remarkable cassette albums which can be a great help and inspiration to you, such as SUPER LIVING. It contains five hours of total uplift and encouragement.

THE BEST OF LIFE

Jesus made a wonderful promise:

If you will confess me before people, I will confess you before my Father in heaven.^{Mat.10:32}

The finest way to say thanks to God for the gift of His *Life* is to share this happy information with others.

SAYING "THANKS!" FOR HAPPINESS

60 SECOND SECRET
DAY TWO

I IDENTIFY with Jesus Christ in a practical way. He is my model of purpose and achievement — my way to the BEST in life.

I know God's original plan was for happiness, health and fulfillment without inferiority or condemnation — like Adam and Eve whom He created.

But they disregarded His plan. That was the origin of human problems.

To save me, **Jesus assumed my wrongs and died in my place. Then He returned with new *Life* from God which He offers to me.**

I *Identity* with Him because, since He assumed my penalty, I am able to receive the new Life of God which He brings into me.

It was *Love's* idea not to let me die in emptiness, but to pay for my wrong, and to restore me to God's lifestyle for which I was originally created.

Now I am at home with God again and He blesses me with life's BEST through Jesus Christ. I have regained dignity. I am restored as God's child.

THE BEST OF LIFE

SECTION THREE

THE PRINCIPLE OF DESIRE

GOOD THINGS ARE FOR YOU

SECTION 3

Part 1 – Dream and Drive for It	73
Part 2 – No Limit to Your Source	75
Part 3 – It Is Right to Desire the Best	78
Part 4 – The Good Life Is God's Idea	83
Part 5 – Walk Tall – Success Is for Now	87
Part 6 – Help Yourself to God's Lifestyle	93
Part 7 – Nothing Is Too Good for You	98
60 Second Secret – Day Three	103

SECTION 3—Part I

Dream and Drive for It

Y OUR YEARNING POWER is more important than your earning power.

People who win in life concentrate on what they desire and ignore any limitations they may face.

1st: *Dream* beyond what seems possible to you.

2nd: *Desire* what you dream about.

3rd: *Drive* for your dreams.

Desire more than the average person settles for. A common characteristic of all winners is, they deeply desire to win.

The force of intense desire in you has a miraculous way of releasing powerful energy, creativity and an almost supernatural pull toward what you yearn for.

What do you want out of life — with all of your heart?

Is it wrong to desire to *do* things — to *be* somebody — to *have* something?

THE BEST OF LIFE

Helen Keller said, "We can do *anything* if we desire enough to do it, and if we stick to it!"

Religion has emphasized surrender, humility, suffering and poverty; it has sanctified resignation, submission, relinquishment and abandonment, but it has neglected the virtues of positivism, development, faith, productivity, success and accomplishment.

Common sense tells us that God did not intend the wealth He created in this world to be monopolized by those who ignore Him. He created it for the pleasure, the usefulness and the fulfillment of those who honor Him and walk with Him.

If you can accept that fact, you are ready for the third secret.

SECRET NUMBER THREE

SINCERELY DESIRE the good things God has created in this world. Believe they are placed here for you—in Partnership with God, to *enjoy* and to *use for the betterment of your world.* Know that *your desire* for good is *God's desire* being expressed *in* and *through you.*

God says: *Listen to me and you will have a* **long, good life.** *Carry out my instructions, for they will lead you to* **real living.** Prov.4:10,13LB

SECTION 3—Part 2

No Limit to Your Source

A PRIMITIVE VILLAGER who scratches the soil with a sharpened piece of wood does not know to desire a steel plow. Once he hears about it, new ideas fill his mind. His ambition is fired. He sets himself to acquire better tools—and a *better* life.

The purpose of God's love plan in the Bible is to show you His *better* way.

Every good gift and every perfect gift is from above and comes from the Father.^{Jas.1:17}

The reason this book is in your hands is because God wants you to know that it is not wrong to desire progress and better living. You are born to enjoy life's BEST.

Hooked up with God, there is no limit to your source for fulfillment.

From the day God created Adam and Eve in an environment of abundance, happiness, health and fulfillment, He has never changed His mind about people.

You were born to live in God's dream, with His lifestyle. You have the miraculous capacity that no other creature has—to think and plan, to ponder and imagine, to believe and progress.

When you recognize God in you and discover that His desires for you have never changed, you begin to dream a new dream—to envision the lifestyle God created you for.

You begin to **rise, to climb and to grow.**

As your new vision gets clearer, that dream **creates deep yearning, deep *desire* for life's BEST and you begin to dare to tackle life, to harness the abilities in you and to go for the top.**

The Bible teaches that God rewards faith.

Faith is *desire* turned Godward.

Have faith in God's dream for you.

Let your desire soar to the level of God's desires for you.

Miraculous changes will begin to take place in you.

God wants you to realize that within you is the possibility to shed the cloak of failure, to escape the negative syndrome of discouragement, to break with the demoralizing dogmas of defeat, to get out of the boredom of conformity and to go

NO LIMIT TO YOUR SOURCE

for life's BEST—whether the "average" person does it or not.

One of the most vital facts you will discover is that God wants you to have good things—the BEST in life, but He must wait, until you *desire* **them,** before He can give them to you.

When a blind man cried out to Jesus, He stopped and asked him, What do you desire for me to do for you? He desired his sight and he received it.

That is the way God works. He desires that you have and enjoy His BEST. But until you desire what He desires, He must wait to give it to you.

Jesus said to a woman who intensely desired Him to heal her daughter—and who **would not give up:** *Be it as you desire.*[Mat.15:28] And the girl was healed.

*When you delight in God, He gives you the **desires** of your heart. You will inherit the earth. God will exalt you to inherit the land.*[Psa.37:4,9,34]

Religion "spiritualizes" God's blessings. It promises that when you get to heaven, you'll be rich.

God's desire is that you *inherit the earth*—NOW. He created it for you to enjoy and to use in **this** life.

SECTION 3—Part 3

It Is Right to Desire the Best

WHEN YOU get God's viewpoint and see how He dreams and plans life in abundance for you, you will no longer be downcast. You will rise up and claim His BEST in life.

The true message of the Bible is *Good* news.

Let me share with you three blessings from God which are *Good*:

1. Peace with God is *GOOD*.

    You were never created for guilt and fear.

    God's love plan for you offers inner peace and tranquility.

    He wants you to have that happiness, but He waits until **your desire** matches **His desire.**

2. Physical health is *GOOD*.

    You were never made to suffer pain, disease or disability.

    God's love plan for you includes healing and soundness.

IT IS RIGHT TO DESIRE THE BEST

He yearns for you to walk in His boundless health. But He must wait until you desire His health in you.

3. Material prosperity is *GOOD*.

You were never created for poverty and deprivation.

God's love plan for you includes prosperity, success and abundant living.

He wills all of His abundance and blessing for **you**. But He must wait until you tire of poverty. When the fire of desire burns in you for His lifestyle, then things begin to happen for you.

Jesus gave you a stupendous promise:

What things so ever you desire, when you pray, believe that you receive them, and you will have them.^{Mk.} 11:24

God has given to you and me the equivalent of a blank check. You are free to fill it in, and that is what you will do when you accept His opinion of you and you begin to desire the *Good Life* that He created for you.

Religion has focused on the negative side of human desire so much that people are impregnated with the idea that *desire* is carnal and must be suppressed.

When I researched what theologians had to say about *desire*, I found volumes written about the

evil of desire. It is condemned, judged, censured and penalized.

I knew that to desire riches or wealth or any other thing out of greed, jealousy, avarice or lust was wrong and destructive.

I knew about Ahab's greed for Naboth's vineyard and how he was so consumed that he died there.

I knew about Joseph's brothers selling him because of greed and jealousy, and of the humiliating result of their deed.

I knew about David's lust for Bathsheba that caused him to sin before God, and the deep remorse that consumed him.

I knew about the rich man who heaped his wealth to consume it in riotous living and how his soul was required of him.

I knew about Judas and his self-destruction over greed and lust for a measly thirty pieces of silver.

I knew hundreds of reasons to warn about **evil** desire. But I know very little in theology that encourages people to **desire** the **good** things that God has created on this planet.

Religious piety and negativism about anything material has practically obstructed the positive viewpoints of the abundant life.

IT IS RIGHT TO DESIRE THE BEST

It is nonsense to believe that God's wealth on this earth is placed here for unbelievers to control. God created it for us to enjoy and to use in His love plan for people.

But since He will not go against your will, He must wait until you dare to *desire* life's BEST.

Many years ago I learned that if I want what God wants, then that desire is holy and good, and I will have it.

What does God want? I will show you in a four-point, mini-résumé of His love plan:

1. He wants what He wanted in the beginning. He wanted Adam and Eve to be happy, healthy, productive, and to live in abundance.

2. Then Satan tempted them. They rejected God's integrity, and forfeited the lifestyle and riches which God created for them.

3. But God loved people too much to see them languish in poverty, loneliness, guilt and deterioration.

4. God gave Jesus, His Son, to come and assume the penalty for your sins. He made only one condition: If you would believe on Him, you would be justified as though you had never sinned. Then God could live in you again, **and all that had been forfeited would be restored to you, and you restored to God.**

See your *Self-Value*, **made in God's image.**

THE BEST OF LIFE

Identify with what Christ did for you and believe that you receive God's life again.

Desire what God has restored to you. Get the BEST out of life.

It is not wrong to *desire* what Jesus died to provide.

If He paid for it, He desires that you have it.

That makes it right for you to *desire* and claim God's BEST.

Realize that *your desire is really God's desire being expressed through you.*

The measure of what you allow God to be, or do, or have in and through you depends upon the intensity of your *desire* to be or do or have.

SECTION 3—Part 4

The Good Life Is God's Idea

YOUR DESIRE DEPENDS on your knowledge of God's desire.

He desires for you every blessing He originally created for human beings on this earth.

Jesus died to redeem and restore you to God. He justified you from all of your past, and brought you back to God as though nothing ever stood between you and Him.

A child said it this way: "I'm justified—*just-as-if-i'd never committed sin.*"

That is God's Love plan. Why?

He wants to give this world back to you, to rule, to dominate and to enjoy. He accomplished that when Jesus assumed the judgment for all of your sins.

Now God offers everything to fulfill your happiness, prosperity, health and abundant living. *All* [things] *are yours, and you are Christ's; and Christ is God's.*^{1Cor.3:22-23}

If you believe in God's love plan, you can have whatever you *desire.*

All things are possible to anyone who believes. ^{Mk.9:23}

What things so ever you desire, believe that you receive them and you will have them.^{Mk.11:24}

*The **desire** of the righteous will be granted.*^{Prov.10:24}

Delight yourself in the Lord and He will give you the desires of your heart.^{Psa.37:4}

Because of sermonizers who stress the negative side of desire, people usually practice suppressing their ambitions. They reject ideas of success and dampen all desire for a better life.

One of the cardinal doctrines of Hinduism is to suppress all desire for any blessing, or status, or happiness, or success in life. It teaches that we are the product of fate; that whatever state we are in, we are to accept it with resignation.

Buddha taught that human persons could achieve a level of mental control where all desires in life would be neutralized and that the very root of desire would die. He called this "Nirvana" or **Desirelessness.**

But the very yearning for the state of **Desirelessness** is in itself **DESIRE.** In fact, it is so intense that one may spend a lifetime struggling in des-

THE GOOD LIFE IS GOD'S IDEA

perate mental search of achieving this paradise of neutrality. It is like trying to cure a headache by getting rid of the head.

We are created with *desire*.

David said, *My heart and my flesh* **cries out** *for the living God.*^{Psa.84:2}

My soul **thirsts** *for God, my flesh* **longs** *for Him.*^{Psa. 63:1}

Our spirits **yearn** for God, for peace, for tranquility, for meaning and for achievement.

Our flesh **desires** the physical and material provisions God has created for us — water, food, air, comforts, success, wealth, abundance, health, happiness and fulfillment.

If those **desires** are suppressed and not allowed to motivate us, we will die in nothingness and emptiness, without purpose or significance.

As God-people, we are not created to be *Nobodies*.

We are heirs of God, joint-heirs with Jesus Christ.^{Rom.8:17}

We are heirs of the Kingdom of God which He has promised to them that love Him.^{Jas.2:5}

We *are* what God *is* in us.

As He IS, so ARE we in this world.^{1Jn.4:17}

The very principle of *Desire* is vital to faith.

THE BEST OF LIFE

To *believe* for something is to *desire* it.

To *pray* for something is to *desire* it.

Prayer is *Desire* turned heavenward.

When desire comes, it is a tree of Life.^{Prov.13:12}

A tree bears fruit when it is alive. The fruit of Life is the abundance of blessings and provisions on this earth that make life full, fruitful, enjoyable and productive.

The *Good* Life is God's idea.

The desire of the righteous is only good.^{Prov.11:23}

When God is alive in you, your *desires* are His *desires*—they are good.

SECTION 3—Part 5

Walk Tall—Success Is for NOW

R ELIGION, IN ITS MANY BRANDS, invariably links *poverty* with godliness, *suffering* with piety, *burdens* with humility and *lack* with holiness.

Emerson, the great American philosopher, says that from the time he was a lad, he wanted to write an essay that would deal with traditional theology which indoctrinates people *against* desiring material success, achievement, and prosperity.

In his inimitable way he said that real life, as people live it, "is ahead of theology and that people know more than the preachers."

Then he explained how a preacher talked about life and the Last Judgment as though every issue would have to await its outcome until then. By this doctrine the preacher ignored the fact that you reap what you sow and get what you strive for, even here in this life.

THE BEST OF LIFE

Mr. Emerson was shocked at the preacher's doctrine for he emphasized that only the *wicked* should be successful in this world and that *good people* should prove their humility and piety by living **lives of misery.**

But then the preacher extolled the fact that God would balance the scales at the great Judgment Day. **Then,** and not before, the *wicked* would get their deserved misery and the *righteous* would inherit riches.

But it was all spiritualized. There was nothing for the righteous here and now — in this material world.

In other words, Mr. Emerson said, the preacher applauded riches for the righteous — *in heaven,* but deplored the thought of material prosperity for them *here and now.*

> He said, in essence, the preacher is teaching the Christians to say: "In this material world, we will submit and suppress our desires and live like paupers, while the wicked revel in their sinful material luxury.
>
> "But *once we get to heaven,* we will no longer cower in submission, suppression and deprivation. We shall stand up and *revel in all of the riches that the wicked have here on earth.*"
>
> In other words, "It is a sin to be rich here and now. We who are pious shall not sin now, but we shall sin in heaven; we would like to sin now, but we shall get our revenge later."

WALK TALK—SUCCESS IS FOR NOW

To young Emerson, this was nonsense. Though he understood little about the Bible, it seemed illogical to him that the wicked should *prosper* and that the righteous should *be poor*. Why not the opposite?

The *Good* News *is* the opposite.

For what purposes will the righteous need silver and gold in heaven—other than to pave the streets or perhaps to form solid building blocks for mansions?

Now—here on earth is where the wealth God created can be put to work for the good of life and the good of people.

God does not need the treasures He placed on this earth. He has plenty in heaven. He put it here for you and me to have and to enjoy and to use.

One of the greatest sins might be to refuse to discipline ourselves, apply our talents and achieve material success—here and now, when it can mean so much in helping people.

Angels announced Christ's coming by saying, *We have glad tidings of great joy for ALL people. Behold a Savior is born!* Lu.2:10-11

A *Savior* from what?

From the judgment of our sins, sure.

But also from the curse of deterioration, self-deprecation and insignificance.

THE BEST OF LIFE

From sickness and disease, from poverty and failure, from mediocrity and humiliation, from disobedience and death.

Jesus came as a Savior from the negativism of religion that condemns, demoralizes, threatens and negates human personhood.

Religion has always been cruel; esteeming laws as being more sacred than lives.

Jesus healed a poor man with a withered hand. The religious crowd yelled: It's the wrong day! Leave his hand crippled! Respect the Sabbath! [Mk. 3:1-6]

They cared more for their law than for a poor man's crippled hand.

Jesus raised a man from the dead who had been in his tomb for four days. The religious crowd never glorified God but recoiled and took counsel to kill Jesus, lest the people follow Him. [Jn.11]

They were so preoccupied about their control over people's minds and the absoluteness of their religious doctrines that, even the restoring to life of a man who had been dead for four days never affected their dogmatism. They preferred to ignore the miracle and to kill the Master rather than to risk losing their manipulating influence over the people.

They brought a woman to Jesus who had been taken in the act of adultery. The religious crowd wanted to stone her to death for breaking the law.

WALK TALK—SUCCESS IS FOR NOW

Jesus treated her like a lady and restored her self-esteem by forgiving her.^{Jn.8:4-11} That is what He did for you and for me.

Jesus came across a naked maniac—a wild man. The religious crowd had no interest in him, but left him to his torment.

Jesus restored his mind and gave him a position of honor. He sent him to ten towns of the Decapolis to represent Him personally.^{Mk.5:1-20} What an honor!

Jesus met an unclean leper. The religious crowd left him to his fate. But Jesus cleansed him so that he could have honor and dignity as a respected citizen again.^{Mk.1:40-45}

Jesus never, ever put anyone down—except religious people who used their religion to put people down.

Religion is usually a put-down—a standard by which one is judged or condemned. **But Jesus** Christ is a *Lifter* of people, a *Healer* and a *Restorer* of human persons.

He wants to restore your faith in life, if circumstances have broken your will.

If you are poor, He wants you to have hope and to believe the *Good* News that good things in life are for you.

If you have been blind to your value, to your potential or to the possibilities around you, Jesus

THE BEST OF LIFE

Christ will open your eyes to see a dozen solutions to problems you thought were insurmountable.

Your ears may have been stopped. Perhaps you missed the answers in life. The Lord will miraculously open your ears and you will hear what counts for life's BEST.

You may have been demoralized until you withdrew in failure and humiliation. Jesus will stand up inside of you and cause you to walk tall in life, and succeed where you failed before.

His message is *Good* News.

He is saying to **you:**

> **You** are a *Somebody*.
>
> ***You*** *are the **salt** of the earth.* Mat.5:13
>
> ***You*** *are the **light** of the world.* Mat.5:14
>
> *Follow me and I will **make** you.* Mat.4:19
>
> *Your sins are **forgiven**.* Mk.2:5; Psa.103:3
>
> *Rise up and walk.* Lu.5:23 Never hang your head in shame again.
>
> *Stretch forth your hand.* Mk.3:5
>
> R-e-a-c-h out — beyond yourself.
>
> *Only b-e-l-i-e-v-e.* Lu.8:50
>
> *Have f-a-i-t-h. All things are possible.* Mk.9:23

He gives hope to the hopeless and power to the powerless; He is good to all who come to Him and call upon Him. *Desire* the *Good* Life.

SECTION 3—Part 6

Help Yourself to God's Lifestyle

TO BELIEVE IN GOD is to believe in *Good*!

For God to live in you, He wants good things to abound in your life. You cannot separate God from His *Good* Life.

God *desires* that you experience these three blessings that are provided by Christ:

1. **God wants you** *at peace.*

If you feel guilty and fearful, remember that Christ assumed your judgment because He desires that you have peace with God.

2. **God wants you** *healthy.*

If sickness or weakness affects you, **desire** His health in you. Want what He wants. He never made people sick. He never told anyone that suffering and pain would glorify Him or make the sufferer any more holy.

He always touched people and gave them health. That is His desire for you.

3. God wants you *happy and prosperous.*

If you face material problems, remember that God created all of the wealth of the world, not for the monopoly of unbelievers, but for the usefulness and pleasure of His people.

If God did not want you to possess and use and enjoy the riches of this world, why did He put them here?

It is right for you to *desire* the material blessings God has put within your reach, for you to prosper, for you to have a nice home that pleases you and to drive a nice car, or to have whatever good things give you pleasure.

It is right that your clothes look nice, befitting someone who walks with God, that you prosper and that your family enjoys the ***Good*** life.

All that God created for His children, in the beginning, is now restored to you through Jesus Christ.

Now the next move is yours. *Desire* what God offers.

Jesus saw a crippled man who had been unable to walk for 38 years.

God wanted that man to be healed. But did the crippled man want to be well?

HELP YOURSELF TO GOD'S LIFESTYLE

Jesus asked him: Do you desire to be made whole?
Jn.5:6

He asks that of you, now.

> Are you **dissatisfied** with life as it is?
>
> Do you **want** a better way?
>
> Do you **desire** a fuller life?
>
> Are you **willing** to be prosperous and successful? Are you willing to assume the responsibility of administering wealth and success for your own good and for the good of people?

The crippled man blamed others for his 38 year plight. He said that no one would help him to get well.

Jesus said, in essence: Help yourself! Get up! Carry your bed! Walk!

The man got up and walked and was whole again.

That is what God says to you and to me.

Decide what you *desire* and resolve to possess it! You can *have* or *do* or *be* anything that you *desire*.

Through ideas and aspirations which He plants in you, in *seed*-form, God in you is desiring to produce the harvest of abundance which was His original dream for you.

Through you, God wants to make a better world *in* you and *around* you.

THE BEST OF LIFE

But until you *desire* what God desires, His goodness cannot materialize in you.

This principle of **Desire** is vital because your action is motivated only by *what you want*.

When there is no desire, no choice is made, no decision is taken, no action is performed.

Without the "want to" there is no "will to".

If your desire is suppressed by religious negativism teaching you that to desire better things and a better life is wrong, then you will waste your life and die in resignation and pious failure.

You will never fulfill the purpose God created you for as His expression of life, happiness, health and prosperity among people on this earth.

You will be like so many who have bound themselves with an oath of poverty. God never planned for anyone to do that. He planned prosperity.

It would be good if you would decide today to take an *Oath of Prosperity* and say:

- "I *vow* never to be poor and indigent again, since my Father created the wealth of this planet for me to enjoy.
- "I *vow* never to be unable to reach out and lift others in need.
- "God is in me and He is rich.
- "I *vow* to always appropriate His BEST in life so that I can enjoy His abundance myself, and I can share His abundance with others in need."

HELP YOURSELF TO GOD'S LIFESTYLE

*The Lord is my shepherd; I will **not** want... My cup runs over.*^{Psa.23:1,5}

That is the lifestyle God created you for.

Dare to break with the bondage of religious negativism. **Desire** God's *good* things—His BEST in life.

SECTION 3—Part 7

Nothing Is Too Good for You

ONLY WHEN YOU DESIRE what God desires can He begin to produce it in and through you. You must know that God wills His BEST for you.

*No **good thing** will He withhold from them that walk uprightly before Him.*^{Psa.84:11}

*I wish **above all things** that you may **prosper** and be **in health** even as your soul prospers.*^{3Jn.1:2}

Jesus said, *I have come so that you may have **Life**, and that you may live in **abundance**.*^{Jn.10:10}

*Instead of shame and dishonor, you will have a **double portion of prosperity** and everlasting joy, realizing that you are a people God has blessed.*^{Jer.33:6,8-9}

You are God's child, so the *good* things He has created belong to you. What do you want to *have*, to *be* and to *do*?

Do you desire better health? A better home or car or job? Companionship? Better relationships with people? A keener awareness of God? More happiness and fulfillment? More money? Greater influence? A happier marriage? More love?

After you have decided what you really *desire*, then write it down and look at it. Begin to see yourself with it. Read your list out loud, every day.

See yourself in God's family with His riches and power and love at work in you and through you.

- Health is *good*. Physical vigor is for you.
- Prosperity is *good*. Riches are for you.
- Success is *good*. Achievement is for you.
- Love and happiness are *good*. Fulfillment in life is for you.

Believe in these *good* things.

Believing is a form of *desiring*.

Prayer is verbalizing your *desires*.

Desire has been called the fire which produces the heat which generates the steam of your will.

When your desire joins with *God's desire* and your will blends with God's will, then God's love power begins to create life's BEST in you.

Let a deep resolve form inside of you that says:

I am through with failure, mediocrity, sickness and poverty.

I am through with jealousy, resentment, fear and guilt.

THE BEST OF LIFE

I am through with loneliness and disappointment, with bills and unpaid mortgages.

The fire of desire is burning in you for a better life, better health, more love, greater success, a closer relationship with God, prosperity, peace and happiness.

Recognize that those desires are *God working in you to will and to do His good pleasure.*^{Phil.2:13}

The first principle to help you get the BEST out of life is to discover your *Self-Value*, the fact that you are created in God's image, for His lifestyle and purpose on this earth.

The second principle is to *identify* with what Jesus did in your place. He assumed the judgment for your sins so that you can be at one again with God like you were created to be.

The third principle is to *know* that God's love plan is only *Good* news; that health, happiness, peace, prosperity and fulfillment are God's *Good* blessings provided for His children. So it is right for you to *desire* the BEST in life.

Jesus said: *The works that I do, you will do also.*^{Jn. 14:12}

That is because He has come to live in you.

Let the real Jesus stand up in you and come alive!

Whatever Jesus is, He is ***in you!***

NOTHING IS TOO GOOD FOR YOU

Everyone He touched was made better, richer, healthier and more successful.

He touched lepers and they became clean.^{Mk. 1:40,41}

He touched blind eyes and sight was restored.^{Mat. 9:29}

He touched crippled and lame people and they walked.^{Mk.6:55-56}

He touched weary and demoralized people and they received new life.^{Mat.14:36}

He touched people with fever and they became normal again.^{Mat.8:15}

He touched people with fear and they were confident again.^{Mat.17:7}

He touched deaf mutes and they could hear and speak.^{Mk.7:33}

He touched wounded people and they were instantly healed.^{Lu.22:51}

That is what He yearns to do *in you*.

So dare to *desire* His BEST.

Your desire is Him yearning in you.

You and God are connected. So…

Resolve to claim God's BEST for your life!

THE BEST OF LIFE

60 SECOND SECRET
DAY THREE

SINCE I AM CREATED like God and since He is now alive in me, *my* desire for good in life is *His* desire expressed through me.

It is right for me to *desire* to be, to have and to do the good that God created me for.

Happiness, success, health and prosperity are God's original plan for me. He has never changed His mind. His love plan is my blueprint for life's BEST.

My *desire* is my *faith* turned heavenward.

I will never allow religious piety and negativism about material blessings to stifle my desire for God's abundance. No member of His family is created for mediocrity or poverty.

I believe in God's plan of Love that restored me to Him, so that now, my *desire* is His *desire* at work in me.

I believe in *good* and desire *good* because I believe in God. It is right that I enjoy His BEST.

THE BEST OF LIFE

SECTION FOUR

THE PRINCIPLE OF DECISION

YOUR POWER SECRET

SECTION 4

Part 1 — You Are In Control	107
Part 2 — You Are Deciding for Yourself	110
Part 3 — How Much Is Enough for You	113
Part 4 — A Beggar Can Become a Master	117
Part 5 — You Are a Branch of God	119
Part 6 — You and God Win Together	124
Part 7 — God Depends on You	127
60 Second Secret — Day Four	131

SECTION 4—Part I

You Are In Control

THE FOURTH VITAL PRINCIPLE to get the BEST out of life concerns the use of *your Power Secret.*

You alone control it. No one but you can use it. It is indispensable to your success.

In this section, you will discover this *Power Secret* and you will be amazed at how easy it is to use, and how quickly it will put you out front.

You are ready for this discovery because you have taken the first three steps.

FIRST: You have *discovered your Self-Value*. Without that, you might spend the rest of your life in mediocrity and inferiority, and never know the self-esteem and fulfillment God planned for you.

SECOND: You have *Identified with Jesus Christ* who restored you to God so that there is nothing between you and Him. With Him living in you and at work through you, you are linked by heritage to all that God *is*, and therefore nothing is impossible for you and Him together.

THIRD: You have dared to *desire the Good Life* that God created here for you, and you have recognized that your desire is God's desire being expressed through you. Therefore you reach out with faith and confidence that it is right to desire the good things of life.

These first three principles depend upon your *Power Secret* that you alone control.

SECRET NUMBER FOUR

YOUR POWER SECRET is your right of choice and your ability to decide **what portion in life** *you will resolve to possess;* **what you will** *settle* **for; what level you are** *content* **with;** *how high you want to climb; how rich you want to be; to what extent you want your business to grow;* **what kind of lifestyle gives you** *fulfillment;* **how** *long* **you want to live;** *how much power* **you want to control;** *how much respect* **you want people to have for you and** *what goals you want to reach.*

YOU ARE IN CONTROL

You—and no other person, organization, influence or agency—have control over your own *choices* and over the *decisions* that you make in life.

For it is God who works in you, inspiring both the will and the deed, for his own chosen purpose. Phil. 2:13

God in you gives you the *desire*, the *opportunity* and the *power* to be, to have, and to do as much as you want.

He leaves the *decision* up to you. You—and you alone are in charge.

SECTION 4—Part 2

You Are Deciding for Yourself

DECISIONS AND CHOICES are verbalized by two of the shortest words in the English language: "Yes" and "No." And the Bible urges us to use these words judiciously.

Say only "Yes" when you mean yes, and "No" when you mean no.^{Jas.5:12}

T. T. Munger says, "The heaviest charged words in our language are those briefest ones, 'Yes' and 'No.'"

People who have left their mark upon the world have been decisive.

Those who are irresolute, always lingering between two opinions, not knowing which course to take, have no *self*-control and are doomed to be controlled by others.

Decisive people do not wait for favorable circumstances nor submit to opinions or influences which negate or demoralize human value.

YOU ARE DECIDING FOR YOURSELF

Decisive people create circumstances. They establish trends. They bend opinions and make them serve positive purposes.

The *indecisive* are always at the mercy of those with whom they last talked. They never belong to themselves but are in the control of whoever captures their attention.

Like a twig or a chip floating near the edge of a stream, they are caught by every weed or bush and are whirled in little circles while their energy is dissipated and their strength is wasted.

The winner in life is a **Decider.**

Winners are well informed. They make clear choices then they resolve to put those choices into action. Like Caesar, they commit all and burn their ships behind them so that retreat is made impossible.

Satan himself cannot stop such a one from possessing the BEST out of life.

The only power Satan can ever have over you, to break, discourage, demoralize, destroy or defeat you is through the negative suggestions or ideas that he can plant, or use someone to plant, in your mind.

Your **Power Secret** of **choice** and the **right to decide** for yourself what measure of life you will settle for, is the power that no one can take from you.

THE BEST OF LIFE

It is not circumstances, but your *choices*, and *decisions* that determine who you *are*, what you *have*, what you *do* and where you *go* in life.

Daisy, my wife, said, "Every morning when I get up, I choose to be happy, to savor life and to make it count for me, for people and for God."

That is why she was always an inspiration, an achiever, a positive influence around the world.

SECTION 4—Part 3

How Much Is Enough for You

Y OUR DECISIONS define what you want in life.

You can decide to win if you choose to win, desire to win, and are committed to win.

You can never fail until you choose and decide to give up.

Decisions and choices are taking shape in you as you read this book.

The law of sowing and reaping guarantees that you will reap the harvest of each choice or decision you make and of each thought you think.

Your life is the sum total of your choices and decision.

Amazing things start happening in life when you decide and choose what portion in life you resolve to possess.

- *Ideas* begin to come to you as to how you can reach out and achieve whatever you have decided upon.

THE BEST OF LIFE

- *Opportunities* come your way that were not available before.
- *People, organizations, companies or businesses* will be there to help you at the right time and in the right place.
- You will discover *new friends* whose cooperation will be available and vital to you.
- Fears and doubts will vanish like dirty smog.
- You will become aware of the new you who becomes successful, valued and respected.
- Vitality, strength and enthusiasm will swell up inside of you.

What portion of life will you *decide* to possess? What are your limits? Are you worthy of the BEST? In your opinion, what do you deserve?

To answer these questions, practice the awareness of the first three secrets I have shared with you:

FIRST: *Your Self-Value,* your dignity as a creation of God, made in His image.

SECOND: *Your identity* with Christ, restored to your rightful place with God where there is nothing to condemn or intimidate you.

HOW MUCH IS ENOUGH FOR YOU

THIRD: *Your desire* to *be* and *have* and *do* what God wants, and the realization that those are *God's desires being expressed through you.*

What are His limits inside you? How much is He worth, living in you? What does He deserve as He lives in you? How much is too much for Him?

Can God be separated from His power when He comes to live in you?

Is God any different in you than the way you think of Him in the Bible?

Does He lose His power and miraculous ability when He comes to live in you? Does He reduce Himself to your standard, or does He raise you to His standard?

How much of the goodness and abundance and beauty of this planet will you allow God to share as He lives in you?

Will you limit Him by the measure of your opinion of yourself? Or will you measure your opinion of yourself by the measure of God in you?

The Bible says, *behold the kingdom of God is within you.*^{Lu.17:21}

God's kingdom is everything that God is — His nature, His power, His love, His health, His wealth, His abundance, His ability, His virtue, His righteousness and His life.

THE BEST OF LIFE

All of that is in you when you let God come home to live in you.

Kingdom means "realm" or "reign" or "domain." Wherever God reigns, no other power can dominate.

Jesus came preaching the reign or dominion of God in people's lives.^{Mk.1:14}

Nothing could stand before Jesus. Sickness, weakness, leprosy, impossibilities, even death yielded when Jesus Christ came to a life.

He was called **Emmanuel,** *which means* **God with us**.^{Mat.1:23}

All things are ***possible*** *to the person who believes.*^{Mk.9:23}

Decide to turn those possibilities into realities. They are no good to you as "possibilities." You can enjoy them only after you and God transform them into material realities, in the *here* and *now*.

SECTION 4—Part 4

A Beggar Can Become a Master

OUR WORLD IS MARKED at every level by people who had no advantages, little or no money, no help and no means of achievement. But they sensed destiny at work in them.

They became aware of their own value and they tackled impossibilities with decision and faith. And they never quit. They succeeded.

To them, every problem became an opportunity, every obstacle was turned into an advantage and every difficulty became a growing experience.

A man by the name of Sanford Cluett found a way to keep cloth from shrinking. That discovery brought him over five million dollars a year in royalties alone.

Henry Ford believed in the knowledge he had and decided: I will build a car cheap enough for anyone to drive and own. He never quit and that

THE BEST OF LIFE

idea brought more wealth to him than any other person of his time received.

A man by the name of Raymond Yates listed over two thousand inventions that were urgently needed at the time.

The knowledge to solve those needs, plus thousands of current ones, was and is in God and He is in *you* and in *me*. So our part is to proceed and to get the BEST out of life.

You and God can meet those needs and that achievement can help take you to the top.

You hold your *Power Secret*.

Week after week, in factories, offices and businesses, millions of people continue to resign themselves to the sterile drudgery of tradition because they have accepted the status quo. They have never used their brain power to think creatively and discover a better way.

By realizing the value of a human person and the potential of anyone who thinks, decides and acts, a beggar can rise to become a master.

SECTION 4—Part 5

You Are a Branch of God

A BUSINESS MAN was praying about the masses of people on the earth who are still unaware of these truths. He asked God: "What are you going to do about it? Are you going to let them die?"

He said God answered Him:

"Son, I have done all I can do. I gave you Jesus. I gave you His Name. I gave you His power, His love, His authority. Now it's up to you!"

You see, the kingdom of God is within you.

So look to God and to His kingdom within you to make every *possibility* a *reality.*

When Jesus talked to the searching, wondering multitude, He said, *Seek first the kingdom of God and His righteousness and all of these **things** will be added unto you.*^{Mat.6:33}

In other words, 1) When you know God has come home to live in you and to work through you; and 2) when you know nothing is between you and God, then you get life's BEST because you realize that it all belongs to you now, as God's co-worker.

It is your right to choose to accept God's kingdom and His righteousness, and to walk as the God-person He created you to be.

Or you may choose poverty, insecurity, fear, sickness, unhappiness, loneliness and depravity.

The decision is in your control.

David chose God's plan. He says:

I will keep Your statutes. I have chosen the way of truth. I have stuck by Your testimonies. I will walk at liberty; for I seek Your precepts. I have said that I will keep Your words.^{Psa.119:8,30-31,45,57}

These statements indicate *choices* which would not be bargained, *decisions* which meant total commitment to God's way — to His ideals.

God says: *I set before you life and death, blessing and cursing: therefore, **choose life** that both you and your seed may live.*^{Deut.30:19}

Choose you this day whom you will serve... As for me and my house, we will serve the Lord.^{Josh.24:15}

When you say "Yes!" to Christ living in you, terrific things begin to happen.

I am the vine, you are the branches.^{Jn.15:5}

YOU ARE A BRANCH OF GOD

You are a branch of God's power and love, of His creativity and abundance.

Everything that is in the vine comes up *into* you and is manifested *through* you.

When you abide in me and I in you, you bring forth much fruit.^{Jn.15:5}

That is the success life. That is the way to get the BEST out of life.

Fruit bearing is success living.

Reproducing what you *are* is bearing the fruit of your life. When God lives in you and is your life, the fruit that you bear is God's life in a human person.

Your life is hid with Christ in God...Christ is your life.^{Col.3:3-4}

Christ is in you.^{Col.1:27}

Christ lives in you.^{Gal.2:20}

It is God who works in you.^{Phil.2:13}

You will know that you are in me, and I am in you.^{Jn.14:20}

Hereby you know that you dwell in God and He in you.^{1Jn.4:13}

He abides in you.^{1Jn.3:24}

Now you are God's own.^{1Pe.2:10}

THE BEST OF LIFE

You are an heir of God, and a joint-heir with Christ.
Rom.8:17

You are the temple of God.[1Cor.3:16]

God has done all He can do. It is your move to choose what God chooses; and when *your* decision joins *His* decision, that releases His love and power within you to manifest His abundant living at your house.

You are a *branch* of God. He is alive in you. As His life pushes up through you, you bear Godfruit. The proof of what God is, shows up in you.

With God at work *in you,* you go from blessing to blessing. *You bear more fruit.*[Jn.15:2]

Getting the BEST out of life, for yourself and for others, glorifies God.

By this the Father is glorified, that you bear much fruit.[Jn.15:8]

But it all depends on your willingness to use your **Power Secret**—your inalienable right to *choose* and to *decide* how much and what of life you will resolve to experience.

Failures are simply the casualties of the world of thought. You only fail when you *think* failure and *decide* to accept failure.

To fail, you must first **quit**. To *quit*, you must *decide* not to continue.

YOU ARE A BRANCH OF GOD

You are much bigger than anything or anyone who tries to stop you. Never give attention to impossible situations, problems or obstacles.

As fast as difficulties loom in your way, transform these tough problems into opportunities to get ideas for solving them.

Nothing is a greater advantage to you than a problem, once you draw on God and His wisdom to solve it. You then have *expertise that is marketable*. It is ability that others will pay to benefit from.

Since most people do not try to solve their own problems, they search for a specialist. You can be that *specialist*!

What's more, you can charge a good price for your services and people will gladly pay it.

So decide to do what has produced millionaires for centuries:

Find a problem and solve it.
   Find a desire and fill it.
Find a need and meet it.
   Find a hurt and heal it.

SECTION 4—Part 6

You and God Win Together

SINCE GOD IS AT WORK *in you* and you have chosen and decided to get the BEST out of life, problems and impossibilities are the material to assist you on your way to success.

You and God can solve *anything. Greater is He that is in you than he that is in the world.*[1Jn.4:4]

Solve your problems and
you will solve the problems of others.

Lift your lifestyle and you will lift others.

Love yourself and you will love others.

Believe in your value and
you will believe in the value of others.

When you practice the consciousness of God's power and mastership in you, you will accomplish the really big things in life. You will produce "much fruit" that will glorify God and bring His BEST to you and to others.

YOU AND GOD WIN TOGETHER

A common piece of steel cannot draw a feather's weight to itself. But when it is magnetized, it can lift ten times its own weight.

Negative people cannot lift negative people.

Down people cannot raise down people.

Only "up" people can lift down people.

Only "strong" people can help weak people.

Your *Power Secret* can change your world.

If the world around you does not satisfy you as it is, you and God can re-create it.

1. *Choose* the idea of what you want.
2. *Discover* the power of God at work in you.
3. *Believe* in the creative force of God to do anything.
4. *Write* down and repeat often, what you want.
5. *Desire* it deeply, believing that your desire for good things is God's desire in you.
6. *Decide* on what in life will satisfy you.
7. *March forward*, with God at work **in you,** until your world is transformed.

Moses decided on his course in life. He made a *choice*.[Heb.11:24-29]

He purposed to allow God to work in and through him, and a burning bush experience so affected him that he transformed two million slaves into a powerful nation for God.

125

THE BEST OF LIFE

What a loss to society, if Moses had not chosen God's way and decided that his people *must not be slaves any longer*!

Their success depended on Moses' commitment. Only when *they* won, did *Moses* win.

In company with God, he never wavered, because he had made a choice, and he stuck to his decision.

When you align your choice with God's choice and your decision with His, you and God win together. No power or opposition can stop you and Him as partners.

Your WILL or desire, aligned with God's will or desire, defeats all opposition.

SECTION 4—Part 7

God Depends on You

WHEN LINCOLN ENTERED the Black Hawk War, he went as a captain but returned as a private. His business failed and the very tools he depended on to make a living had to be sold to pay his debts.

The first time Lincoln tried for the Legislature he was defeated, as he was in his first attempt to become a Congressman.

When he tried for the office of Commissioner of the General Land Office, Lincoln failed again. Then he failed when he tried for the Senate. He also failed to get nominated as Vice President.

But Abraham Lincoln never did quit. He became President of the United States and is recognized as one of the greatest leaders our nation has ever had. His decision to excel never weakened.

Thomas Edison, in his 10,000 attempts to invent the light bulb denied that he ever failed. He just found thousands of ways it would not work. He was committed. He and God never quit.

The electricity was there all the time. Edison allowed God to help him harness it.

President Grant, at 39, was chopping and delivering wood for a living. But his choice was noble and his decision was lofty. Nine years later, he was elected President of the United States.

Thousands of so-called "nobodies" have chosen the *good* life, decided on the BEST, and have risen to lead nations, build fortunes and establish institutions for the betterment of humanity.

When you choose, decide and act with God at work *in* you, nothing can stop you and Him together from succeeding.

Twenty-five thousand cases of failure were analyzed. The glaring evidence showed that lack of decision was the principal cause for defeat in every case.

Four out of five graduates from our schools of higher learning have not yet decided what they want out of life. Statistics prove that, at the age of sixty-five, only one out of a hundred graduates will be rich.

Several hundred success stories were analyzed. In all cases, those who had succeeded had made clear choices, had informed themselves as well as

GOD DEPENDS ON YOU

possible, then had decided and committed themselves, and had achieved their goals.

The majority of people who fail are deeply affected by, and therefore subject to the opinions of others.

There is nothing more plentiful, and of less value than the opinions of people who are not successful.

You have a brain and a mind of your own. You are at the controls of the greatest *Power Secret* on earth for **your** life—your right of choice and decision.

Manage it or be manipulated by the whims, the opinions, the negative influences of other people.

You are far too vital and of too great a value to be subjected to or manipulated by others who, once you are down, will walk off and leave you and forget that you ever existed.

God is not that kind of a partner.

He *believes* in you, *trusts* you, *wills* His BEST for you and *identifies* with you.

He makes your house *His palace*; he *depends* on you, *created* you, *reaches out* to you and *lives* with you.

All things are possible with God [in you].^{Mat.19:26}

Choose what you want in life and *decide* to experience it. Use your own *Power Secret*.

THE BEST OF LIFE

Think for yourself and value your own ideas.

Accept all that God is in you and believe in His love, His power, His presence and His abundance.

Act on the fact that God is *in you* and reach for the stars.

Stand up tall, like God.

March to the sound of His music.

Go to the top with Him!

60 SECOND SECRET
DAY FOUR

GOD HAS GIVEN me a *Power Secret* which I alone control. It is my right of choice, my ability to *decide* how much I want out of life, how high I want to climb, how rich I want to be, how long I want to live, how much power I want to have or what goals I want to reach.

I inform myself, I set my targets and I achieve my goals because I choose to win. I have *decided* that God and me cannot be losers.

I recognize God at work in me.

He does not reduce Himself to *my* standard. He raises me to *His* standard.

I have chosen and have *decided* to get life's BEST because I *am* God's BEST. He created me in His likeness—first class all the way. His Mastership is in me.

The only person who can limit me is the one who makes my decisions.

I choose life, success, happiness, health and prosperity. I have *decided* to say "Yes" to God's BEST because that alone glorifies Him, fulfills my life and makes my world better.

T.L. and Daisy Osborn, dressed in national attire, arrive at the stadium grounds of another city for another great gospel crusade as they had done in nearly 80 nations prior to the demise of Daisy on May 27, 1995.

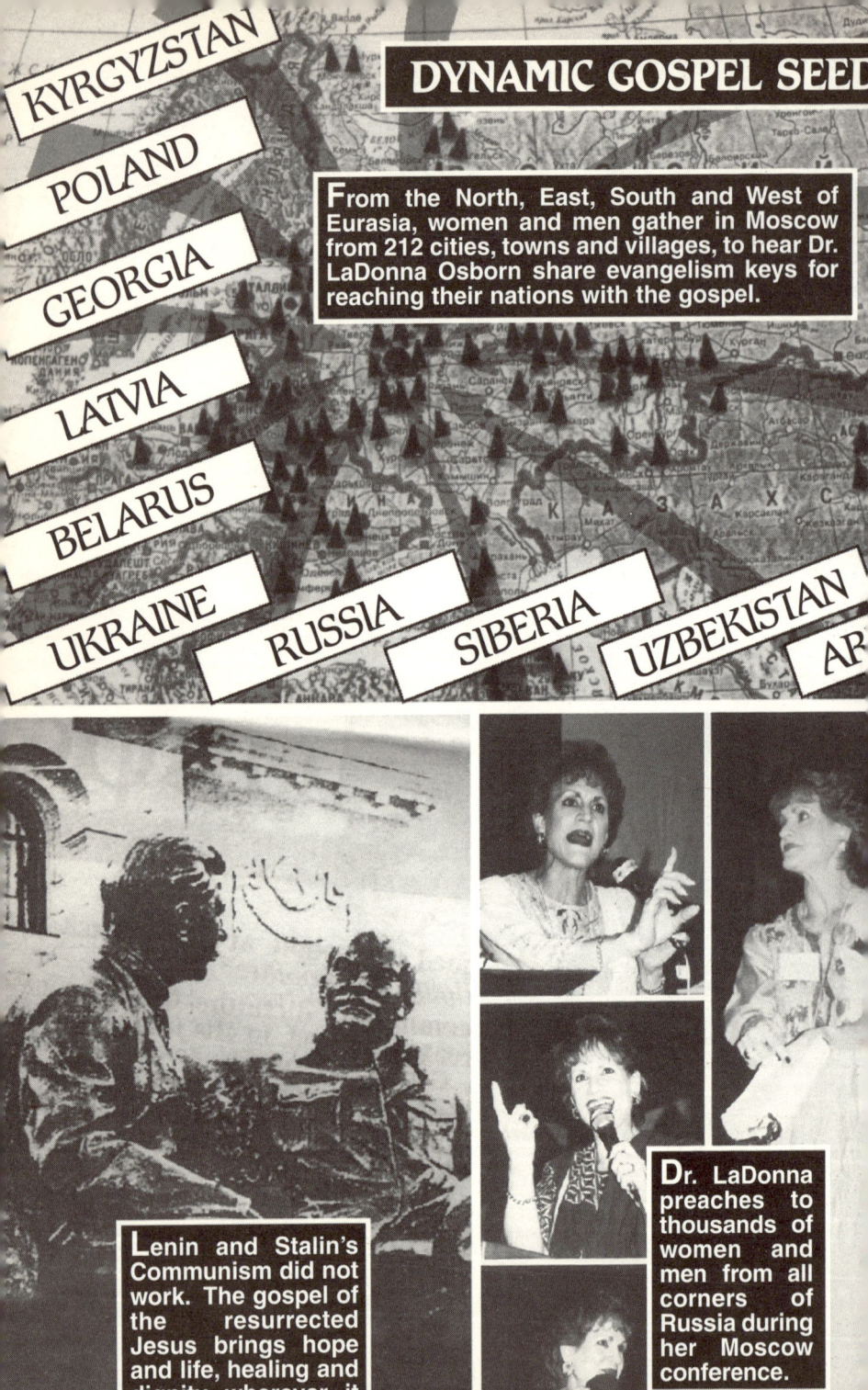

DYNAMIC GOSPEL SEED

KYRGYZSTAN • POLAND • GEORGIA • LATVIA • BELARUS • UKRAINE • RUSSIA • SIBERIA • UZBEKISTAN • AR...

From the North, East, South and West of Eurasia, women and men gather in Moscow from 212 cities, towns and villages, to hear Dr. LaDonna Osborn share evangelism keys for reaching their nations with the gospel.

Lenin and Stalin's Communism did not work. The gospel of the resurrected Jesus brings hope and life, healing and dignity wherever it is proclaimed and demonstrated.

Dr. LaDonna preaches to thousands of women and men from all corners of Russia during her Moscow conference.

OWN ACROSS EUROPE

In Russia alone, there are 36,000 totally unreached villages. In Kazakhstan, there are 14 million people who have never heard of Jesus. The harvest is RIPE! The time is NOW!

KOLSKIY PENINSULA
BASHKORTOSTAN
TATARSTAN
KHAKASSIA
ABKHAZIA
KAZAKHSTAN
UDMURTIA
KARELIA
URAL REGION

LaDonna's focus is reaching the unreached, and establishing them as vibrant ambassadors of Christ, expressing His love-power to others.

Pastor of large, church & Bible school in Siberia.

Woman believer learns truths that build her faith in God.

She writes feverishly to avoid missing any nugget of truth.

From their soulwinning youth to their global ministries that spanned 54 years, T.L. and Daisy Osborn's multi-faceted world ministry made the gospel known to millions in nearly 80 nations, motivating people to discover *The Best of Life* through faith in Jesus Christ.

ON THE GO LIFTING PEOPL

After Daisy's demise in 1995, the Osborn daughter, Dr. LaDonna, assumed the direction of their global ministry as Vice-President & CEO. She and T.L. continue ON THE GO for souls in nations around the world, sometimes together but usually on two national fronts at once.

SECTION FIVE

THE PRINCIPLE OF WEALTH

YOUR BIG CONNECTION

SECTION 5

Part 1 — There Is Plenty for You 143
Part 2 — You Are Tapped into God's Wealth 147
Part 3 — See Yourself in God's Class 151
Part 4 — The High Purpose of Material Plenty 156
Part 5 — God Has Big Ideas for You 160
Part 6 — You Are Seeded for Abundance 166
Part 7 — God's Generosity 170

    60 Second Secret — Day Five 181

SECTION 5—Part I

There Is Plenty for You

GOD IS GOOD, liberal, limitless, bountiful!

For you to get the BEST out of life, discover the generosity, the affluence and the liberality of God.

Discover that the only *Life* God planned for you, or anyone else, is the *Abundant Life*.

From the beginning of creation, God set Adam and Eve in the middle of total affluence, beauty, health, wealth and happiness.

Having created the world, He commanded the waters and the ground to *bring forth a-b-u-n-d-a-n-t-l-y.*^{Gen.1:20}

He blessed every living thing that He created and said, be fruitful and m-u-l-t-i-p-l-y.^{Gen.1:21-22}

That was God's idea for human persons.

God's Will for you is no different than His Will was for Adam and Eve.

When Jesus Christ came, He re-emphasized God's dream. He said, *I have come that you might*

THE BEST OF LIFE

have **Life** *and that you might* **live in abundance.**
Jn.10:10

Our Lord Who has created such abundance would not withhold that material plenty because He wills that His people be poor.

He Whose power and love are unlimited would not refuse to manifest His blessings when His children call upon Him for help. He is not so miserly that His followers must beg and plead for needed blessings. He is abundantly generous.

You have this book in your hands because you liked the idea of reaching out with biblical faith to experience the BEST in life.

I have written it to help you discover the principles that have lifted so many out of mediocrity into a life of blessed abundance.

It is beautiful to see someone transcend apathy and learn to experience achievement.

God is glad every time someone is motivated to walk out of the darkness of negativism into the sunshine of His rich life.

The world is better every time someone discovers that God wants human persons to be healthy, successful and materially blessed.

It is beautiful to see the spiritual, physical and material blessings that take place in people who recognize God's goodness.

With this fifth secret or principle which I am going to share with you, you can realize every good thing that you ever hoped for.

- You can know freedom from worry and fear and lead a supremely happy life.
- You can realize physical health and enjoy a good life of loving ministry to God and to people.
- You can be more productive on your job, or establish a new enterprise that will succeed. You will have a more positive influence on people and be respected in your community.
- You can discover the unlimited source of creativity that is in you.
- You can discover your big connection with God's abundant supply and be blessed so that you can be a blessing to others.
- You can turn your daydreams into realities. You can discover the happiness, success and health that are within your reach.

Now I share with you the fifth secret to help you get God's BEST in life:

SECRET NUMBER FIVE

RECOGNIZE the wonderful fact of God's *riches*, that *He has created such an abundance on this planet that there is plenty for you* of whatever you can need or desire, and that *it belongs to you because God created it for the material blessing of His children who do His Will.*

THE BEST OF LIFE

The abundance that God has created in this world proves His generosity. He has decked your world with splendor, beauty and unlimited material plenty.

God placed man and woman in a veritable paradise of bounty, generosity and material wealth. And it belongs to you as your estate!

Never allow religious sermonizers to whittle you down to the level of an unworthy indigent before your Heavenly Father.

You are made to enjoy God's abundance. He has created plenty for you. There is no shortage, no limit.

No good thing will God withhold from them that walk uprightly before Him.^{Psa.84:11}

*For as you know Him better, He will give you, through His great power, everything you need for living a truly **good life**. He even shares His own goodness with you.*^{2Pe.1:3LB}

SECTION 5—Part 2

You Are Tapped into God's Plenty

NOTHING IS IMPOSSIBLE, or too good for you and God together.

Shortage exists only in your mind; limits exist only in your thoughts. God knows no scarcity.

You are created (then *re*created) to be *one with God*, sharing all that He is and has.

You are a member of His royal family. He wills His abundant blessings for you.

This may sound too good to be true, but it is a fact: You are like the followers of Christ who were caught in their boat by a menacing storm. All of the time that they were frightened and felt helpless, Jesus was present in their boat—asleep.

He is there in your life too, but He does not assert Himself unless you call on Him.

Frantically, the disciples awakened Jesus and He stood up in their boat. When He did, the storm was stilled, and they reached their goal.

Let the living Christ *stand up inside of you!* Call upon His power that is resident within you. Recognize Him in your boat. He is adequate for any situation.

When God came home to live *in you*, through Christ, He made you a partaker of all that He is.

God's divine power has given to you all things that pertain to Life...[with] *exceeding great promises by which you can be a partaker of the divine nature.*[2Pe.1:3-4]

Recognize the wealth of God that is yours. See your big connection with Him! He has created abundance everywhere and He has done it for your prosperity and success. Refuse, forever, any tendency or influence that identifies you with poverty or non-achievement.

If you consider yourself to be among the poor, or the incapable, or the sickly, or those who seem inferior, or the non-achievers, it is only because you have not recognized the rich material blessings of God that is yours.

Religious tradition teaches that it may be God's plan for you to live in poverty, helpless, defeated, inferior and humiliated; that such conditions may be a blessing in disguise to teach you humility and godliness; that you must not resist sickness and

YOU ARE TAPPED INTO GOD'S WEALTH

disappointment which may draw you closer to God; that you may be required to lead a meager existence; that physical suffering, financial limitations and submission to defeat and failure can be the influences which develop virtues of humility and holiness in you.

But those circumstances are a form of hell on earth, and you don't have to go through hell to get to heaven. They are foreign to God's dream for you.

Jesus talked about *treasures* which moths and rust corrupt and which thieves steal.

The *treasure* or *wealth* that God brings to your life cannot be taken from you. No thief can steal it. No moth or rust can destroy it.

The abundance that God gives to you is spiritual wealth, but it will produce material wealth at your house, because when you know that you are in rapport with Divine Royalty, nothing is too good for you.

The only way you can be *poor or unworthy* is not to recognize Christ and His power at work in you.

The only way you can feel *guilty or afraid* is not to recognize that Jesus assumed your judgment and left you justified forever before God, with no reason to ever sense guilt, fear or condemnation again.

THE BEST OF LIFE

The only way you can ever feel *inferior or subservient* is not to recognize your self-value as one of God's children, made in His own image.

You have been redeemed by Christ and you are a believer. You are restored to His level and status of *Life*. Now His quality becomes your quality. His wealth becomes yours. He created plenty for everything that you can desire, need, use and enjoy.

There is no shortage for His royal family. You do not have to be poor to be holy like Christ. He became poor like you so that you can be rich and holy like Him.

Though he was so very rich, yet to help you, He became very poor, so that by being poor He could make you rich.[2Cor.8:9]

SECTION 5—Part 3

See Yourself in God's Class

WHEN YOU DISCOVER God's *Kingdom in you*, you begin to recognize that you were not meant to be poor or inferior. You are in God's class of being. All that He *has* and all that He *is*, is yours.

Deep within your heart, you have never wanted to submit to inferiority, failure or poverty. Something inside rises up to throw off those slave-shackles.

Jesus Christ is standing up inside of you right now, wanting to throw off sickness, suffering and lack, and to cause His power and material abundance to blossom in your garden of Eden where He lives with you.

He is saying to you: *"Stand up with me and let's experience the BEST in Life."*

He taught you, as His follower, how to pray.

THE BEST OF LIFE

FIRST: Jesus said to begin each prayer by honoring your Father — *Our **Father** in heaven.*^{Mat.6:9}

That means to recognize your *Self-Value* as a child of God, related to Him, a member of His royal and divine family.

SECOND: Jesus said to recognize the family name — ***Hallowed** be Your name.*^{Mat.6:9}

You belong to the hallowed family and carry the hallowed name. Never disgrace that name by acting as though you are inferior or that you are obliged to live in mediocrity.

THIRD: Jesus said to recognize that God is at work *in you* — *Your **Kingdom** come. Your Will be done, in **earth** as it is in **heaven**.*^{Mat.6:10}

In other words, acknowledge the reality of God's Kingdom functioning in you. Agree with God's Will that He wants to do *good* things in earth (in us) the same as in heaven.

When you say, "*Your Kingdom come, Your will be done,*"^{Mat.6:10} you are not surrendering or begging. You are declaring, agreeing and speaking in faith saying, "*Yes, Father, I agree; may all that You are be manifested in me, here and now!*"

SEE YOURSELF IN GOD'S CLASS

The wealth of God is in His kingdom. His kingdom is in you. You are in Him. You cannot be poor, or fail or be ordinary.

*God will supply all of **your** needs according to **His** riches in Christ Jesus.*^{Phil.4:19}

The blessing of the Lord makes you rich.^{Prov.10:22}

The Bible abounds with God's goodness, His generosity, His abundance and with proof that the wealth of this planet was put here for those who believe in Him.

There will be golden streets in heaven. God also created gold here on earth for us.

There are unfathomable gems and precious stones in heaven. God also created an abundance of them here on earth for us.

There are fruit bearing trees in heaven. God also created them here on earth for us.

Why, then, the religious idea that wealth is evil and poverty is holy?

Throughout the Old Testament, men and women of God associated wealth, happiness, success and abundance with the blessing of God.

*The Lord daily loads us with **benefits**.*^{Psa.68:19}

*When you seek the Lord, you will not lack any **good** thing.*^{Psa.34:10}

THE BEST OF LIFE

Both **riches** and honor come from God, and [He] reigns over all.[1Chr.29:12]

The Lord will make you **plenteous** in goods... He will open His good **treasure** to you...and will bless all the work of your hand.[Deut.28:11-12]

God brought you into a **plentiful** country, to eat the **fruit** and the **goodness** of it.[Jer.2:7]

Your barns will be filled with **plenty**.[Prov.3:10]

You will eat in **plenty** and be satisfied.[Joel.2:26]

Jehoshaphat had riches and honor in **abundance**.[2Chr.18:1]

Hezekiah had exceeding much riches and honor, treasures, silver, gold, precious stones...all manner of pleasant jewels; storehouses...possessions in abundance: for God had given him **very much substance**.[2Chr.32:27-29]

God has given riches and **wealth**...this is the gift of God.[Ecc.5:19]

The Lord has pleasure in the **prosperity** of His servant.[Psa.35:27]

Abram was very **rich** in cattle, in silver, and in gold.[Gen.13:2]

The blessing of the Lord makes **rich**.[Prov.10:22]

Blessed is the one who fears God...**Wealth** and riches will be in that house.[Psa.112:1,3]

Believe in the Lord your God...So will you **prosper**.[2Chr.20:20]

Jesus came and taught us that all of God's wealth, happiness, peace and the abundant *Life* is for everyone who believes in Him.

I have come that you may have Life and that you may be in ***abundance.***^{Jn.10:10-French Bible}

The apostles urged followers of Christ to expect and to claim the BEST in life.

*I wish above all things that you may **prosper,** and be in health, even as your soul prospers.*^{3Jn.1:2}

SECTION 5—Part 4

The High Purpose of Material Plenty

FOR A FEW HUNDRED years after New Testament times, Christians succeeded and prospered.

Then they began to lose the vitality of the Christian message. Reality changed to formality. Religion became a ritual. Liturgy became more vital than life.

Consequently, church leadership became political and that led to the monopoly of money and wealth by the religious hierarchy.

Sanctimonious, ecclesiastical leaders dominated city and state governments and manipulated people for the benefit of the powerful church monopoly.

During this early epoch, clever religious spokesmen, contriving to manipulate society's wealth, originated new doctrines and began to teach: to be holy like God, one must choose poverty and ma-

THE HIGH PURPOSE OF MATERIAL PLENTY

terial penury; one must hand over his or her property, money and material holdings to Christ, via the Church.

To read their doctrines, you would think God was poor and destitute, and that He needed every earthly thing that His people possessed.

Exactly the opposite was true.

God created the abundance of wealth on this planet for the use and enjoyment of His children.

Since that early epoch when religious teachers manipulated the scriptures for their own purposes, the Dark Age doctrine that *poverty equals holiness* has persisted.

The facts are that money and material prosperity are blessings of God for His children, so that people can be partners with Him in lifting and blessings others.

God is *good* and He wills *good things* for His children. *The Lord will make you* **plenteous** *in goods, in the fruit of your body, in the fruit of your cattle, and in the fruit of your ground.*^{Deut.28:11} God wills abundance for you.

Naturally, material wealth, hoarded and selfishly guarded, never produces happiness.

But when you recognize *The Big Connection*, that you are in rapport with God, that His Kingdom is in you and that you and He are united in His

THE BEST OF LIFE

Love-plan to lift, to heal, and to bless people, then material wealth has Godly purpose.

The idea that has made millionaires is to find a need and meet it, to find a desire and fill it, to find a problem and solve it or to find a hurt and heal it.

When you taste the blessing and the joy of being able to help and to lift others, then God's wealth in your life has divine purpose. This gives meaning to love, to power and to material blessings.

I am not attempting to deal with the negative side of material plenty, of the evil of loving money for its own sake, of the cancer of greed, of the destructive power of pride and superiority nor of the disease of financial lust for power.

This aspect is already emphasized by religious writers everywhere. I trust you to believe that I am balanced.

I could write a book on the negative aspect of wealth, the suffering it has caused and the ruthlessness and human cruelty of money-power.

My emphasis here is the positive aspect of God's wealth for His children. My purpose is to encourage you to believe for life's BEST *so that you can lift others as you lift yourself.*

THE HIGH PURPOSE OF MATERIAL PLENTY

You can never know life's BEST with the cancer of greed, lust for material wealth consuming you from within. That is not God's BEST.

But recognizing your own value and that the wealth of this planet was created by your Father and was put here to be used in His Love-plan for people—*that* generates value and purpose for God's BEST in your life.

God wants you to know *The Big Connection* in order to do *big* business with Him, to live the *big* life, to utilize His *material provisions* to lift your *big* world on a *big* scale.

SECTION 5—Part 5

God Has Big Ideas for You

GOD'S KINGDOM IS *big* business.

You are part of a *big* Love-plan.

David said, *When I consider God's heavens, the work of His fingers, the moon and the stars which He has ordained, [I am amazed].*^{Psa.8:3}

Why did our Lord make billions of stars? Wouldn't a few thousand have sufficed? If He wants you limited or impoverished on this earth, why such an extravaganza in the heavens?

How could God want you to live in deprivation, when He created so much wealth all around you?

Why did He make such huge mountains and so many of them—full of treasures? What purpose would it serve if His followers are to live in scarcity and insufficiency?

Why did God create such vast oceans and fill them with such wealth, if He wants His people to exist in meagerness?

GOD HAS BIG IDEAS FOR YOU

Why did He create so many huge trees? Why such vast deserts, such lush jungles, such enormous plains and such rich valleys? And why so many of them?

No parsimonious, tightfisted God could ever have created the abundance that you live amidst.

*Who is so **great** a God as our God?* ^{Psa.77:13}

*How **great** are His works!* ^{Psa.92:5}

***Great** are His tender mercies.* ^{Psa.119:156}

*The Lord has done **great** things for us.* ^{Psa.126:3}

***Great** is our Lord and of **great** power.* ^{Psa.147:5}

When you consider God's *Big Connection,* your mind stretches, your imagination enlarges, and you think *big* thoughts—you get *big* ideas. And when you think *big,* then you talk *big* and you act *big.*

Throughout our world ministry, whenever my wife, Daisy, and I faced impossibilities and our faith was tested, we got away from limited horizons and went to the mountains, or to the desert, or to the ocean and contemplated the greatness and the generosity of our Father. Our minds were s-t-r-e-t-c-h-e-d to God's infinity.

We realized that our Lord had created all of earth's abundance, and we were in His class of being.

THE BEST OF LIFE

Contemplating God's abundance helped us to draw courage and renewed faith to meet our task. We learned to release Jesus within us to stand up tall in our boat and to calm our storm.

Knowing that God has *big* ideas for us, we have always been re-energized to think *big* with Him.

When we were in the Papua New Guinea mountains, teaching those precious people these secrets, I was intrigued by the Pidgin English translation of 1 Timothy 1:12 which, with my adaptation to make it understandable to you, goes something like this:

This Big Fellow that belongs to me, Jesus Christ; He gives me strong power. He thinks I am good enough to do all of His works and He put me in this big work of His. For this I thank this Big Fellow, Jesus, who lives inside me now.

Clearly, the Papua New Guinea people have captured the essence: God has *big* ideas for you and for me.

John 1:12 is a *big* idea: *To all who receive Jesus Christ, God gives the power to become children of God.*

God dares to believe in you enough to transform you into His own child, as quick as you believe on Jesus and welcome Him into your life.

Mark 11:24 is a *big* idea: *What things so ever you desire, when you pray, believe that you receive them, and you will have them.*

GOD HAS BIG IDEAS FOR YOU

God has such grand ideas about you that He commits the honor of His word to see that if you ask Him for anything you desire, and you believe His word, you will have it.

John 14:12-13 is another *big* idea: *Anyone believing in me will do the same miracles I have done, and even greater ones, because I am going to be with the Father. You can ask Him for anything, using my name, and I will do it.*

What trust God puts in us!

David looked into the heavens. He considered how *big* God is. Then he began to *think big.*

That's what you are doing right now.

Someone asked Helen Keller, the renowned blind, deaf and mute author, "Isn't it awful to be blind?"

She answered without hesitation: "Not half as bad as it would be to have two good eyes and never to see anything!"

What a tragedy to live with God in you, to have His Kingdom in you, to be His child, to have all of His material blessings, power and abundance available to you; then to be so indoctrinated by the theology that demands physical suffering and material poverty, that you never rise, claim, enjoy and use the wealth of God's abundance.

THE BEST OF LIFE

A little boy excitedly reported what he had witnessed. He said, "I seen..." and an adult voice broke in to correct his grammar.

He retorted: "It is better to say 'I seen' and see something, than to say 'I saw' and never see anything."

Electricity was here all the time, waiting for someone to get the *big* idea of harnessing it for the good of people.

The air waves, with their miraculous power to carry words and pictures around the world, have been unchanged for millenniums, awaiting our search for and discovery of them for the good of humankind.

Most great discoveries have come from things which everybody thought they knew about, but somebody pondered until the *big* dream was born.

The great fortunes which have made millionaires out of ordinary people have come from opportunities which were available to many but which somebody did something about.

The purpose of this fifth secret, the principle of material wealth, is to help you discover the abundance and the generosity of God who placed you here amidst His created abundance so that you can be happy, healthy and successful.

All of God's created nature is your estate. His wealth is stored here for you. It is abundant.

GOD HAS BIG IDEAS FOR YOU

Your heavenly Father knows that you have need of all these things.^{Mat.6:32}

This fifth secret to getting the BEST out of life is not a *responsibility* thrust upon you; it is your *response to God's ability* at work within you.

SECTION 5—Part 6

You Are Seeded for Abundance

ONE OF THE MOST successful men of this century recounts the speech that his stepmother made soon after she married his father and came to live in their poverty-stricken home:

She gathered the family together and announced that the place they called home was a disgrace and a handicap for the children.

She reminded them that they were all able-bodied and that there was no reason for them to accept poverty. She reasoned that if they remained as they were—resigned to their circumstances—the children would do the same.

Although for the time being, she did not know how they would break out to freedom from poverty, she made it clear that they would make the break successfully, regardless of the time it might take or the price they might have to pay.

With pride she announced that she would see to it that those children would be impregnated

YOU ARE SEEDED FOR ABUNDANCE

with the drive to master poverty, which she regarded as a disease, adding that any time poverty is accepted it becomes almost terminal.

She assured them that, although being born in poverty was no disgrace, "It most decidedly IS a disgrace to accept this birthright as irrevocable."

She reminded them of their fortune to be born in the wealthiest nation on earth, where possibilities abound for any person who has the drive to observe and to accept them. She added that, if circumstances were not favorable, then they would create new and favorable circumstances.

She notified that family that poverty was like creeping paralysis; it would eventually suffocate the desire for success and liberty; it would stifle the drive for an improved lifestyle and would debilitate individual enterprise and aspiration.

She vowed to make sure that those children would become "prosperity conscious", that they would expect life's BEST!

The speech that woman made that day broke the grip of poverty upon that family as it seeded faith for a better lifestyle and started them on the road to *The Best Of Life*.

I believe this book will break the influence of poverty, inferiority, poor health and disappointment in your life forever.

THE BEST OF LIFE

You are being seeded for abundant living. You can do anything that you believe God can do through you. This one *big* fact should make you an eternal optimist.

There is no limit upon you except the limit that you place upon God who lives in you.

As God's child, you are entitled to all of the *good* things that He has placed in your world, so expect nothing but *good*.

Your stomach is made to enjoy and to digest good food.

Your ears are made for the sounds of music.

Your eyes are made for rainbows, green meadows, blue skies and colorful flowers.

Your lungs are made to breathe good fresh air.

You are made for happiness and health, for achievement and abundance. That is your domain.

It is right for you to get a better job, a good home, to enjoy health, to live as a "somebody" with a sense of well-being, of dignity, of accomplishment and of self-esteem.

God has created plenty for you to have all that you can need or desire. He has decked your world with treasures. They are for you. His wealth is your birthright.

I have invested almost sixty years teaching these principles to multitudes in nearly ninety nations.

YOU ARE SEEDED FOR ABUNDANCE

I have observed the disastrous effect that a theology, negative about material blessings, can have upon people and even nations.

It is amazing how many people are programmed for failure and poverty. They have resigned themselves to do without what they want, to never feel good about themselves and to accept their present role as permanent. No one has to do that.

Once these principles are discovered, you and God will transform your world. You will climb out of the *average* category and rise to new levels of success, pride, achievement and happiness.

I have found tremendous fulfillment in sharing these secrets worldwide. It is rewarding to observe how the uplifting influence of these principles help shape a better world for people.

These secrets are already working wonders in you. It is impossible to know them and not be positively affected by them.

SECTION 5—Part 7

God's Generosity

From the Oklahoma Hills to a Hurting World

SOMETIMES IN MY DESIRE to screen out the negativism of society, I get away from it all and get alone with God and nature where I can ponder the generosity and the opulence of our Father's abundant creation.

I love the Oklahoma hills and streams where I played as a child. I love to walk among the strong oak trees, ponder the miracle power of the soil where I worked as a barefooted boy, and walk alongside the clear brooks where I went fishing as a lad.

A Single Acorn

I pick up a single acorn at the base of a huge oak tree, and I hold it in my hands.

GOD'S GENEROSITY

Like David in the Bible who considered the heavens and realized how big and generous God was, I look up at the huge oak tree and I know that it grew out of that small seed. David was awestruck by the heavens.^{Psa.8:3} Jesus spoke of the wonder of growth in the mustard seed.^{Mat.13:31}

All of the technological miracles of humankind could never produce that strong oak tree, or make that tiny mustard seed grow to such proportions. But God did. And it was easy for Him.

There among nature *I receive the message:* The greatest power that exists cannot be measured by a meter, or analyzed, or seen; but it is real and it produces, and *it is at work in me.*

A Handful of Soil

I walk down in the river basin, across the rich field where, as a lad, I planted corn pushing the kernels into the soil with my bare toes.

I bend over and pick up a handful of soil and I consider the wonders of God. Jesus said, *For the earth brings forth fruit of herself; first the blade, then the ear, after that the full corn in the ear.*^{Mk.4:28}

There in my hand is the essence of the very substance that produced the corn we harvested in the autumn, and the "stuff" that produced those huge oak trees that I love so much.

Rich soil! Another element in my world of wealth! God created it—so abundantly.

I Get The Big Idea

I get the big idea. My Father has plenty. He lives in me. We are one. We are rich.

I walk beside the river. I think about the millions of people I have taught or will teach, face to face, across this planet.

God says, *I will open rivers in high places, and fountains in the valleys.*^{Isa.41:18}

I want people to look at God's created abundance that surrounds them and *see* with their own eyes the wealth with which they are connected.

There, away from the plastic, electronic, buzzing, beeping world, *I am hearing God's message of abundance.*

I Pluck A Fern Leaf

I pluck a fern leaf and as I ponder its intricate design and beauty, I am caught away again. *I hear God whisper His message again.*

I ponder the trees, and I observe that each leaf is different. The Lord said: *You will be as a tree planted by the waters, that spreads her roots...her leaf shall be green and...shall not cease from yielding fruit.* ^{Jer.17:8} God's will is always for us to produce abundantly.

GOD'S GENEROSITY

Jesus said: *My Father is glorified, when you bear much fruit.* ^{Jn.15:8} His provisions are always abundant, and He wills that we produce bountifully.

His message is loud and clear.
- Every snowflake is unique.
- Every baby's face reflects Him.
- Every thumbprint is unmatched.
- Every human voice is original.
- And *you* are exclusive in His plan.

As I ponder nature's wealth, I pray that I can help people recognize God's abundance around them; that I can cause them to rid their minds of stingy, negative and poverty-programmed theology and religion; that I can help them discover *The Big Connection* and recognize that material blessings, happiness, health, success and abundance are God's gifts for everyone who believes in Him.

You will be abundantly satisfied.^{Psa.36:8} *You will know the love of Christ...and be filled with all the fullness of God.*^{Eph.3:19} *He will give rain to your seed, so you may sow the ground; and the bread of your increase will be plenteous.*^{Isa.30:23} *He will make all grace abound toward you; that you may always, having all sufficiency in all things, abound to every good work.* ^{2Cor.9:8} *His Will is abundantly above all that you ask or think, according to His power that works in your life.*^{Eph.3:20}

THE BEST OF LIFE

The Miracle of Water

I follow the little stream back away from the river. The water is clear. I can see the fish.

I sit down on a boulder beside the stream and remove my shoes to splash my feet in the cool water like I did in my youth. *And I hear another message.*

Water! A miracle! From the beginning of God's abundant creation, water has been the miracle worker. What stories it could tell if it could talk to us.

Ever since this planet became the habitat for human persons, water has been the life-giving servant to all. The thirst of billions has been quenched by it. It has been transformed into steam to power humankind's mechanized world, then it faithfully returned to its liquid form to serve again. What a rich partner — *water*!

Sewers are cleaned, clothes are washed and thousands of services rendered. Then it always returns to the oceans from whence it is drawn back into the heavens and purified before repeating its cycle of service on our planet.

Water! It is so much like God — never quitting, never ceasing, never retiring and never stalemating.

GOD'S GENEROSITY

No one can create it. No power can destroy it. It always comes back, clean and pure. Without it, nothing on our planet could live.

Jesus spoke of His own Life-giving message: *Whoever drinks of the water that I shall give him shall never thirst; but it shall be in him a well of water springing up into everlasting life.* Jn.4:14

As I pondered the water, I thought of our *Big Connection.* God is at work in you and in me. He is our source. He never quits. His regenerating power lifts, heals, saves and blesses all who reach out to Him. His refreshing is always, pure and clean. It always brings new and everlasting *Life.*

The Sun—Its Energy

I pull my feet out of the water and put on my shoes. The sunshine comes streaming through the trees. I walk out to a grassy slope and stretch out in the sun—and consider. And lo! *Another message of abundance!*

The Sun! What power! What wealth! What an energy source! Without its incalculable energy, that small acorn never could have germinated in the rich soil, and those minerals, mixed with water could never have been converted into that giant oak tree, or yellow corn, or intricate fern leaf, or rich fruit, or beautiful flowers.

THE BEST OF LIFE

I remembered how the prophet said: *But unto you that fear my name shall the Sun of righteousness arise with healing in his wings.*^{Mal.4:2}

Without the sun, the brook where I played as a boy never could have existed and those fish never could have lived. And without the Son of Righteousness in my life, I never could have experienced the wonders of His grace in my own life, and upon so many millions of needy people to whom I have witnessed.

There is so much of HIM shining—so much *energy*, so much *salvation*, so much *healing*, so much *new Life*. The supply is infinite. The hope of our world depends on Him and on His living presence. Without Him, humanity would be trapped in nothingness, emptiness and unfruitfulness.

Without the sun, the wonder of *water* would have been forever trapped in the oceans. Life on our planet could never have existed.

And so it is with God! *I get the message.* So much *sunshine*! So much of *God*! Plenty for me! Plenty for you! No shortage!

A Single Pebble

I get up from the grass and start back to the city. Everywhere I look, everything I see is *pouring out God's message of abundance.*

I stop by the brook and pick up *a single pebble*, and again, *I hear the message.*

GOD'S GENEROSITY

That pebble seems dead and motionless but it is not. It is made of molecules. Inside each one are myriads of atoms, each of which is actually a little universe in itself.

Within every infinitesimal atom are worlds of electrons which move at speeds inconceivable to the human mind.

Within that small pebble, there exists all of the basic materials that one would find if the stars could be examined microscopically.

While that pebble seems dead, it is really a highly organized family of units of endless energy. It is not a solid mass as it appears to be. Each electron is actually separated from another by a space larger than itself.

What a study in life! *That small pebble* looks so ordinary, yet all that is in the universe is at work in it.

I Am A Living Miracle

That makes me think of God at work in me — and in you.

God is one with us. His Life is our life. You and I are His models. All of the creative power and energy that He *is*, is energizing your life and my life, right now. *We are living miracles by the creation of God.*

The power and energy that keeps the sun, stars and earth in their orbits, is at work in us right now. We are part of God's *big* plan.

It is time to recognize *The Big Connection*. We are in rapport with God. We count in His Love-plan!

You are a royal citizen, a vital part of His rich Kingdom. You are identified. You belong to God. He imparts Himself to you and to me. We are energized by Him.

His Message For My World

I have walked with God and have discovered afresh the evidence of His bounty and how much He wants us to recognize His abundance.

Jesus said: *I am come that you might have Life, and that you might have it more abundantly.* Jn.10:10

So after hearing God's message that is so abundant in nature, I return to Tulsa and to my world, to tell humanity that God never created anybody to be poor or worthless, despondent or inferior nor to live without joy, happiness or fulfillment.

I find my way back to my writing library and to my garden, back to the radio or television audiences, back to public platforms out on fields, in stadiums and public parks, back to the nations abroad — back to the millions who long for God's message of abundance.

I return to the world that is hurting and suffering, that is confused and bitter, that is lonely and forgotten, that is poor and needy and that is unfulfilled and unsatisfied.

I have the secrets to help the people of my world to get God's BEST in life.

Seeds in *Word*-form

I take my pencil in hand and, as I write, I see you, dear reader-friend.

I know the seeds of truth which I plant in you — in *word*-form — will germinate and will produce in your life the wondrous fruits of success, happiness, physical and mental health, joy, material blessing and the greatest fruit of all — *salvation, dignity as God's child, self-value as a member of His Royal Family, and the awareness of His esteem for you.*

Jesus said, Everything is possible for a believer. Mk. 9:23 There is no shortage of His energy or ability. You are *connected* with the source that created the universe. Let the living Jesus stand up tall in you.

Know that you are God's special creation, destined for life's BEST because He, in you, deserves it.

So resolve today to get His BEST out of life. His abundance belongs to *you* — is created for you!

THE BEST OF LIFE

His eyes run to and fro throughout the whole earth, to show Himself strong on behalf of those whose heart is loyal toward Him.^{2Ch.16:9}

For You, O Lord, will bless the righteous; with favor You will surround him [or her] as with a shield.^{Psa.5:12} *O Lord, You are the portion of my inheritance and my cup; You maintain my lot.* **Yes, I have a good inheritance.**^{Psa.16:5-6}

60 SECOND SECRET
DAY FIVE

I RECOGNIZE THAT the abundance which God has created is proof of His goodness and great generosity.

There is plenty for my needs and my desires.

Since the wealth of this earth was created by our Father, it is *good* and not *bad*. It was not intended for the monopoly of unbelievers but for the use of those with faith in His *Love-plan*.

It is no disgrace to be poor. It *is* a disgrace to believe in poverty.

God created me for abundance. It is right that I enjoy life's BEST.

I refuse religious bigotry that condemns wealth and sanctifies misery. God created plenty. There is no shortage for His family.

In God's Love-plan to lift, to heal and to bless people, material wealth has divine purpose.

As His partner I vow never to accept poverty, but to stand up and to believe for God's BEST in life because I am part of His *big* plan, and His material blessings are part of my birthright.

THE BEST OF LIFE

SECTION SIX

THE PRINCIPLE OF VISION

REVIEW

THE

NEW

"YOU"

SECTION
6

Part 1 — The *"YOU"* You See Is the *"YOU"* You'll Be   185
Part 2 — Beyond Humanism to Unlimited Miracles   191
Part 3 — Lifted to Dignity and Self-Esteem   196
Part 4 — Forming a New Image of Life   200
Part 5 — Miracles Are Waiting in You   203
Part 6 — Seeing Life's Best at Your House   208
Part 7 — Now I See a Brand New Me   214

    60 Second Secret — Day Six   223

SECTION 6—Part 1

The *"YOU"* You See Is the *"YOU"* You'll Be

THE MIRACLE OF SIGHT must be among the most awesome wonders of life. The delicate mechanism of the eye is astounding. Yet it is not really what you see with. Your brain is what sees.

With your eyes closed in sleep, you may watch entire scenes of faces or places or happenings with such perfect detail that you can never forget them —yet they did not appear in the material world. What you "saw" in your dream, was a vision created by your brain.

You have the ability to see in different ways. Your brain receives the image of what materially appears before your eyes.

Also, you have the power to SEE by forming mental pictures which do not exist materially. You can project positive or negative possibilities, scenes and situations.

THE BEST OF LIFE

Fear or worry is the negative use of your imagination. You project situations which have not occurred and the same feelings are experienced as if they were real—anxiety, headaches, an upset stomach, a rise in blood pressures, acceleration of the heart beat, rapid breathing, constriction of arteries, etc.

If your imagination can be used in negative, destructive ways, you can also deliberately use it in a positive, constructive way and get positive results.

Worry and fear are fed by negative information—by *seeing* negatives scenes. Faith, poise, confidence and assurance are nourished by positive information—by *seeing* positive scenes.

I have trained myself to see God at work in me, to see His faithfulness, His generosity, His power and His abundant *Life*. I see *Him* and I have courage, assurance, peace and happiness.

Some people walk amidst beauty and never ponder it. They live where love abounds but are never conscious of it.

Some walk among the flowers but never smell them. They hear a baby cry, or watch a hummingbird suspended before a lily, but never see God in these wonders.

Human persons are created in God's image, to walk and talk, to live and plan with Him. When

THE "*YOU*" YOU SEE IS THE "*YOU*" YOU'LL BE

He is not welcome, there is a vacuum. Emptiness, loneliness, meaninglessness and insecurity dominate.

The Bible says, sin brings death. Not to see God is a terrible sin. Solomon said, *where there is no vision, people perish.*^{Prov.29:18} When you lose the vision of God, *you are dead!*

I am writing this sixth secret to help you discover the value of your ability to *see,* to *imagine,* to *think* and to draw such a source of strength and power from God at work in you, that nothing can stop you from getting everything you want in life.

An idea, a concept, a thought or a vision is something you see with your mind — a mental picture. Your thoughts are the pictures which you personally *choose* to project in your mind.

The visions which you see and ponder wield an almost miraculous influence upon you and your lifestyle. The phenomenal law of life, irrefuted for centuries, is that *you become whatever you envision.*

Some of the greatest and most helpful books ever written are those designed to underscore this law and its influence upon your world.

I am ready to reveal to you the sixth secret of how to get the BEST out of life.

SECRET NUMBER SIX
(in FIVE STEPS)

FIRST: Get a clear VISION in your mind and spirit of the unique "You" that *God has created and that Christ died to redeem,* with the unlimited potential that His presence in you represents.

SECOND: Gather all of the information you can, from the Bible and elsewhere, to support that uplifting VISION of *the "You" that God made in His own image.*

THIRD: Reject every thought, concept, counsel, image or vision that in any way diminishes, devaluates, demoralizes, depreciates, discredits or depresses *your VISION of the "You" that God made to walk and to talk with Him.*

FOURTH: Refocus and reproject your picture of the "You" created by God and redeemed by Christ, and hold that vision of the new "You" in your mind and spirit *until you forget what the old self was like.*

FIFTH: Become acquainted with that transformed new "You." Believe in Christ at work in your new *being.* Act according to the new, re-created "You." You will actually *become that updated, new "You"* that is now redeemed by Christ and that is at *one* with your Father in heaven.

THE "*YOU*" YOU SEE IS THE "*YOU*" YOU'LL BE

Every page that you read in this book is projecting the picture of the potential new "You" upon your mind and spirit. In that way the seed of the new *"You"* is planted and it is beginning to produce after its kind.

It is affecting the way you will talk and act. You will go out the same door as before, but the world will look different to you.

You will walk down the same sidewalk but the way you walk will change. There will be certainty and decisiveness in your steps. You will carry your shoulders differently. Your health will improve. You will sleep better. People will admire you and you will inspire the best in them.

Whenever you meet or mingle with people in offices, factories, marketplaces, churches, clubs, homes or wherever, they will treat you with greater respect and esteem. They will have confidence in you. You will be more convincing, attractive and likeable.

I cannot over-emphasize how vital your acceptance of this new "You" is. You are a God creature, made in His image, and He wants you to believe in the redemption that Christ has wrought to redeem you.

*Without **faith**, it is impossible to please God.*[Heb. 11:6] Jesus said, *Have **faith** in God.*[Mk.11:22] *Anyone who comes to God must **believe**.*[Heb.11:6]

The Bible tells us that *faith comes by hearing the word of God.*^{Rom.10:17} Your power to *think* is your power to *believe.*

To read the Bible and learn about God's promises is the knowledge that, when fed into YOUR mind and spirit, becomes the basis for *believing.* That is scientific — biblical!

Whenever and wherever the promises of God recorded in Sacred Writ have been believed and acted upon by sincere people, God has made them good, and He will make them good in your life too.

SECTION 6—Part 2

Beyond Humanism to Unlimited Miracles

CHRISTIAN HISTORY is filled with numberless accounts of miracles which people who had faith in God experienced.

During the 20th Century, with the advent of radio, television and satellite communication, the world was made aware of the fact that thousands of miracles were being experienced in the lives of people who *believed in God*, who *trusted* His word, and who *acted* upon His promises.

I am a living witness of this fact today in this century. My wife and I were ministering in India as missionaries back in 1945. We did not know about miracles, so we did not succeed.

Following our return to the USA, we learned the truths of faith in God and the principles of His miracle-Life. We discovered how to get His BEST in life. Then we set out to teach those treasured truths to nations abroad. We have reached millions of people in almost ninety nations of the world. (Be sure to get our unique 512 page pictorial, *The Gospel According to T.L. & Daisy. Nothing else like it has ever been published.*)

Seldom have our audiences been less than 10,000 to 15,000. Usually they number from 20,000 to 50,000 and many times from 75,000 to 250,000 people or more in a single mass meeting.

There are thousands of persons today who are living, walking miracles, and are witnesses of the remarkable changes which have been experienced by those who have attended our meetings and have heard us share these powerful and life-changing truths of the Gospel.

Nations are affected.

Broken families are healed and bonded by a new love.

Alcoholics and *chemical dependents* are totally cured.

Politicians rise to greater success and esteem.

Women discover their value and rise to new levels of leadership and responsibility.

People who were beggars, now run their own businesses.

University students use these secrets and become successful in leadership.

BEYOND HUMANISM TO UNLIMITED MIRACLES

Housewives become business executives, owners and entrepreneurs.

Poor people now live good and prosperous lives.

Diseases and sicknesses are miraculously cured.

The deaf, the dumb, the lame and the blind are healed.

Cancers, tumors and all sorts of incurable maladies disappear.

Defeated people regain self-respect and self-worth.

Loneliness and fear are lost in the glow of new faith and purpose.

The object of this section on "The Principle of *Vision*," is to project in you the picture of the wonderful "You" that God has created, and to inspire you to hold that *vision* until, by His miraculous power, you actually become all that you see by faith.

To achieve this phenomenal transformation, base your *vision* on information that is valid and proven. The BIBLE is the most proven and the most reliable information available anywhere.

Philosophers, psychologists, professors of psychosomatics, of mental science and psychic religions have evolved remarkable statements, clichés, theories and formulas which appear to be helpful, inspiring and productive.

But, without the miracle of being restored to God through Jesus Christ, self-improvement is limited to nothing more than psychological humanism.

While this self-help process of the mind can motivate improvement in lifestyle and circumstances, it cannot touch the supernatural, creative realm of God's domain in you through the redemptive work of Christ.

The realm I am sharing with you in this book is the realm of the miraculous, and it is for you.

Human mental science is an effective energy force, just as the healing power of the human body is a wonder to medical science.

But the secrets I am revealing to you go infinitely beyond humanism and mental science. They relate to God in a super-natural *Life*style.

When you discover the facts of 1) your *identification* with God, 2) your *relation* with His Life-source, and 3) your *potential* with Him at work in you, you realize God's miracle, creative power at work within you, which is actually *His Kingdom in you* and nothing is impossible when you and God become partners.

With God at work in you, ideas that come to your mind which are 1) good for *God*, 2) good for *people* and 3) good for *you*, are messages direct from Him.

BEYOND HUMANISM TO UNLIMITED MIRACLES

If they are *i-m-p-o-s-s-i-b-l-e*, that is even more proof that they are from God because they exceed the limits of humanism and have room for God — they require a *miracle*.

All things are possible if you can only believe.^{Mk. 9:23}

When you dream of God at work in you — of your actual companionship with Jesus Christ, you get a new *vision* of the *new "You"* in a *new Lifestyle* that is as much greater than humanism as the universe is greater than the earth.

SECTION 6—PART 3

Lifted to Dignity and Self-Esteem

THE PICTURE THAT you perceive of yourself, that is projected from the Holy Scriptures, is the seed of God's faith at work in you.

Your power to *think* is your power to *have faith.*

Your *faith* and your *hope* are the *vision* or the *picture* that you see in your mind or spirit, based on what the Bible says. It is the picture that represents the miraculous possibilities that exist with God at work in you.

This new *"You"* is made possible because the principle of your sin has been dealt with by Jesus Christ, in your place. Since He paid the penalty for all of your sins, nothing you ever did can stand between you and God to accuse you, or threaten you with judgment, or fill you with guilt, fear or inferiority.

LIFTED TO DIGNITY AND SELF-ESTEEM

Consequently, the new, restored and recreated *"You"* that God paid so much to redeem, can stand up and become a living representative of Him at work in human form on this earth.

This is the only way God can fulfill His original dream for you.

In that way, *"EMMANUEL"* (*"God with us"* — Mat. 1:23) is re-demonstrated in you as He was in Jesus Christ.

At last, you are at home in God and God is at home in you, which was His original dream for you and for Him.

You become a human being who lives as Christ's representative, an heir of God, a joint-heir with Jesus Christ, with the kingdom of God actually headquartered in you, which is the Temple of the Holy Ghost.

- No wonder, when you review the new *"You"* with God's kingdom at work in you, nothing will be impossible unto you.
- No wonder you do not fail, or live in poverty, or stand in a bread line, or accept shame and abuse, or feel lonely, guilty, fearful or inferior.
- No wonder you should experience the material blessings God has created in this world, for your own provision and for the good of people around you.
- No wonder God planned that you have faith in His Word and that you purpose to experience His BEST in life.

THE BEST OF LIFE

- No wonder when you review the new *"You"*, your lifestyle changes, diseases wither and disappear, marital problems fade and the way you dress, walk, live, talk and think clearly reflects your transformation.

You rediscover the dignity and self-esteem of a human-person in partnership with God.

There is no tragedy like a human being without self-esteem or self-worth, existing without awareness of identity with God; no rainbows, no flowers and no future—nothing but empty existence without meaning.

A blind man sat in a flowered park with a sign around his neck that said: "It is springtime and I am blind!"

What a tragedy to be a God-creature, to have this knowledge available, and never to get the vision of the transformed *"You"* that God designed and values so much.

Traditional religion reduces you to a cowering, unworthy, worm of the dust. God lifts you to the realm of dignity and royalty with Him.

A young Kikuyu tribal girl heard us teach these principles. She was a village "nobody," a Kikuyu female, uneducated, with no cultural worth beyond the dowry her father would collect and the child-bearing and wood-carrying ability for the man who would own her as his wife.

LIFTED TO DIGNITY AND SELF-ESTEEM

Following the teaching that we share during our seminar, Jesus appeared to her in a vision, and told her to go explain the Bible promises to people and to pray for them; that He would go with her and would work through her and bless the people.

Across her nation she journeyed on foot, on bicycle, by cart and by other means of primitive conveyance. A stream of miracles followed that girl until the crowds became so large that policemen had to protect her while she taught and prayed for the people.

She learned what Jesus Christ did for her and how God wanted to live in and through her. She received a new vision of herself, recreated in God's image, with God at work in her through Jesus Christ.

Her ministry has grown until she has traveled across Scandinavia, America and Africa helping people in Christ's name. She was a female *nobody* who was transformed into a powerful woman of God who has been received like a queen wherever she has journeyed with the Gospel.

SECTION 6—PART 4

Forming a New Image of Life

GOD WILL DO wonderful things through you, when you see your potential in Him. As long as you *think* you are a *nobody* and *see* a *nobody* in your mirror, you will walk, talk and act like a *nobody*.

The average person tends toward indoctrination—creeds, guidelines, limits and absolutes which are established by others.

The average person is programmed by culture, religion, educators, family and peers; by television, by the newspaper, by their organization or club or community.

Once others categorize you and fit you into the mold of their making, if you accept their opinion and live like you think they think you should live, that is what I call being indoctrinated. People who submit to this manipulation seldom ever rise beyond the level that is pre-programmed for them by others.

FORMING A NEW IMAGE OF LIFE

Once you are indoctrinated, your mind is fixed and you stop thinking creatively.

This is why religion often stunts personal growth. (I said "religion" — not vital Christianity.)

Many religious doctrines are outdated. Sermonizers limit God to 16th Century English and make Him sound like a prophet from antiquity.

But God is very much alive in the now and has never changed. He speaks your language and is speaking today in many ways, continuing to impress upon you that He values you and wants you to get the BEST out of life.

This book is one of the ways He is speaking to you — right now.

God is trying to get you to *rethink* and to *reassess* who you are, why you are here, what your value is and what you can *be* and *have* and *do* and *enjoy*.

God thinks you are *super*. He created you for miracles, for abundance, for power and energy. But He can never force improvement upon you. You are not a robot. You have the power of choice.

If mediocrity is acceptable to you, that is what you will have. If you want the *good* life, you can achieve it. If it takes excellence to please you, it is there for you.

Your present circumstances exactly match the *vision* or *picture* of life that you hold in your mind.

THE BEST OF LIFE

You may have passing fancies of a better life. Higher thoughts may flicker across your mind. You may glimpse a picture of a better situation.

But the predominating, day-and-night concept of life that you have allowed to take form in your mind exactly matches the way you are living today.

But you and God can change that.

God created you to possess and manage this earth, to be the channel of His power, *to have dominion...over ALL the earth.*^{Gen.1:26-28}

But He must wait until you are willing to think new thoughts, to formulate a new image of life and to see a new vision of yourself based on His love-plan for you.

SECTION 6—PART 5

Miracles Are Waiting in You

WHEN YOU WELCOME the new concept of the new *"You"* that God created, a five-step process begins.

- **1st:** You get the thought or *vision*. You see the *picture* that the Bible reveals.
- **2nd:** You organize the idea into a *Plan*, depending on God to help you.
- **3rd:** You *decide* and *commit* yourself to God's new ideal for you which He originally planned from the beginning.
- **4th:** You initiate *action*, determined to experience what you envision from God's Word.
- **5th:** You *realize your dream* and become what God restored you to be.

The whole process begins when you allow your brain to be re-programmed with new information about a new "you."

The *seed* of that idea from God is as certain to produce *"after its kind"* as wheat seed produces wheat. Cherish that God-given vision. Review that new "*You.*"

Nourish that concept with more and more information from the Bible and from every good, positive source. Review and rethink the facts that you have discovered.

Treasure the music that stirs in your heart. Esteem the image of dignity and nobility that is projected on your mind and spirit.

The *vision* you hold is the promise of what will unfold in your life.

Ideas, thoughts and visions *are seeds*. When they are based on God's Bible Love-plan, they are *miracle seeds*, and they will yield or produce *after their kind.* Gen.1:11-12

A morbid mind filled with sick thoughts will produce a morbid, sick body. Mental discord produces physical discord.

Develop faith in God's Love-plan and in His ideas about you, and you will drive out the devil of pessimism, the great breeder of disease, failure, and misery in human lives.

Take control over the pictures you allow to formulate in your thinking by being sure that they conform to God's image of you.

We behold…the glory of the Lord and are changed into that same image. 2Cor.3:18

MIRACLES ARE WAITING IN YOU

Concepts of weakness, failure or poverty are destructive and demoralizing. They will reduce you to their level. They are your deadliest enemies — vicious thieves of your happiness, health, success and abundance.

Resist as you would demons, the ideas that you are poor, unworthy, limited, weak or inferior. Those ideas are lies! You were born to succeed, not to fail.

When Jesus said, *The kingdom of God is within you*,[Lu.17:21] He was telling you that all of His generosity and creative ability are built into you to guarantee you His BEST in life.

When you understand that your *vision* is *seed-power*, and that seed always produces *"after its kind,"* then you begin to comprehend the power of an idea — of a vision.

Idea-power and vision-power are **seed-power.**

In your own brain are ideas of power just waiting to be born, to grow and to procreate. You have the capacity for over three billion ideas, according to scientists.

Decide to bring some of those ideas into living, breathing existence for you and your world.

It is said that, at best, we use only ten percent of our thinking power. That means that God who is at work in us is being allowed to accomplish, at best, only ten percent of what He created us for.

People campaign for the right of unborn babies to live. What about the potential of unborn ideas? What about the miraculous *you* that God designed and paid to redeem?

You were perfectly born. But education, religion, tradition and peer-influence stuffed you into its own mold, harnessed your brain, programmed your spirit, categorized your worth, fixed your limits and determined your possibilities.

Society brain washed you and manipulated you to serve its purposes. Public tradition and culture cemented you into the category that society chose for you.

But is "society" to blame?

The fact is that you chose to think their thoughts, accept their opinions, live by their standards and submit to their codes for you.

It is strange that you never need the permission or approval of others to be average, or poor, or inferior, or mediocre, or commonplace.

Only when you get ahead in life, or rise in success, or achieve excellence do people think they have the right to control you, to limit you, to dictate how much is enough for you or how high you should rise or how rich you should be.

It is strange that society does not care how poor you are, how little you have; they are not concerned about your debts, your mortgages, your empty pantry, your flat tire or your car that does not run.

Why then should you need their approval to prosper and to experience the BEST in life?

The only influence that can keep you down — or that can advance you, is the choices that you, yourself make, the vision or concept of your own value, the level of life or the goals that you decide upon.

No law or creed, no religion or State can take from you the privilege of reading your Bible and of formulating the vision of the lifestyle that you choose with God's help.

SECTION 6—PART 6

Seeing Life's Best at Your House

IN CERTAIN NATIONS, perfectly born infants are deliberately blinded or their legs and arms are broken, twisted and left to heal in deformed positions. The gods are supposed to be pleased for a member of the family to be crippled and to spend his or her life as a beggar.

Traditional religion often does that to the human spirit. Born into God's family healthy and perfect, the eyes of the mind are blinded to God's miraculous, abundant lifestyle. Attitudes are twisted and warped by pious ideologies and sanctimonious doctrines.

Teachers sermonize about poverty being saintly, about sickness glorifying God, about failure and defeat being virtuous and about submission to commonalty being holy.

The facts are that God created birds to fly, fish to swim and people to be happy, successful, healthy and productive.

SEEING LIFE'S BEST AT YOUR HOUSE

Jesus said, *Blessed are the eyes that **see** the things that you see.*^{Lu.10:23}

God gave you eyes to see with. He created you with the power to envision, to imagine and to see.

And if you cannot see, the Bible says, *God openeth the eyes of the blind.*^{Psa.146:8} He wants you to see, to believe and to have faith.

God told Abraham to **look** as far as he could see and promised him that *whatever he could **see**, he would possess.*^{Gen.13:14-15} That is why He wants your vision clear, so that you can *see* His abundance and possess life's BEST.

A blind Hindu was led to our meetings in South India among some 75,000 people. As I talked about God's love and what Jesus Christ did to redeem us to God, he was astounded. Having never heard the Gospel before, he wept and told God that he believed what I was saying.

The man said that he experienced a sensation like warm water washing his entire spirit, mind and body. Overwhelming peace swelled up in his heart, and when he opened his eyes to look up toward God in thanksgiving, they were as clear as the eyes of a new-born child. God had healed his blindness.

Our eyes are made to see.

Our minds are made to think and to see mentally. We are the only creatures made in God's likeness. We have the almost miraculous power of imagination—to carry a vision in our minds and spirits.

A baby boy was carried to our meeting in Africa. The child was born without eyeballs.

The mother heard our teaching and new faith was born in her heart. Standing amidst some 65,000 people, she listened, then she prayed earnestly to God for a miracle and the child was marvelously healed.

Small eyes formed in the boy's empty sockets, and he could see. Thousands of people swarmed after the mother as she walked through the town to return to her village.

By the following day, perfect, beautiful eyes had been formed in the child's head and he was normal.

For over a year, people trekked to that village to see the boy with the miracle eyes and hundreds believed on Christ.

Almost anyone in the provincial capital of Nakuru could take you to that village because they know about little Simeon.

Daisy, my wife, was in the province two years later on a special mission concerning evangelism in East Africa. So she visited the village to see the lad again and news spread about her coming. So many people gathered that she conducted an unscheduled Gospel meeting for the crowd in that village and many people believed on Christ.

God wants you to have physical eyesight, and He also wants you to learn to *see* spiritually, to *imagine* and to *envision* the wonders of His promises and of His Love-plan for you.

If we can learn to *see* our God-given potential and value *ourselves*, we will *see* and value *others*. Instead of condemning or judging people, we will lift them and help them. In this way God can work in and through us to make a better world.

When Jesus Christ met people, He said or did something to lift them to a new level!

He met a naked, crazy man who ran among the tombs and cut himself with stones. Jesus saw in him the potential of a terrific, personal representative of His miracle power.

Jesus cured the man, clothed him, then commissioned him to go to the ten towns of the Decapolis and witness to the people of the miracle he had experienced.^{Mk.5:1-20}

Jesus transformed a crazy, naked *nobody* into a representative of divine royalty. He can transform any impossibility into a remarkable opportunity in your life.

What we call the *Beatitudes*, in the fifth chapter of Matthew, are ideas expressed by Jesus when He sat down and gave that most inspiring discourse to the common people.

His lesson was an outline of nine ways that they could be beautiful, happy, blessed and lifted. There was no hint of accusation, judgment, condemnation or put down!

Jesus never put anybody down! — except the religious people who *used their religion to put other people down.*

Poor and needy people always thronged Him and He always uplifted them, blessed them and made them feel valuable.

Jesus said, You are the *light* of the world. You are the *salt* of the earth.

He told the helpless cripple, *Rise up and walk!* He never wanted anyone to crawl or cower or to feel inferior.

To the man with the withered hand He said, *Stretch it out!* He never wanted anybody withered or paralyzed or unuseful.

The religious committee was ready to stone a woman to death because they had caught her with a man in the act of adultery.[Jn.8:3-11]

Jesus said to Himself: *"I will make her feel like a lady again."* He saw in her the wonderful human being His Father had created. He knew condemnation would not heal her. He forgave her and sent her away with dignity and self-esteem.

SEEING LIFE'S BEST AT YOUR HOUSE

Jesus received an unclean leper. The pious crowd was shocked and withdrawn. They saw a curse, a blight in society. But Jesus saw a gentleman who needed help and compassion!

The Lord is not looking at how many sins you have committed, the wrongs that you have done to yourself, to your loved ones or to your community.

He will never put you down, accuse you, berate and demoralize you.

He is coming to you through this book...

- Showing you your infinite value;
- Showing you how you can use your right of choice and decide to believe in His Love;
- Showing you that His created wealth witnesses that He wants you materially blessed;
- Showing you that with Him living in you, nothing will be impossible for you and Him;
- Showing you that He desires life's very BEST at your house.

The only power that can keep you from being all that God designed you to be, is your own thoughts, your own opinions, the pictures you see of yourself, and the vision you hold.

SECTION 6—PART 7

Now I See a Brand New Me

THE TRAMP IN THE PARK sees the chauffeur-driven Rolls Royce go by, carrying the man with the tall silk hat, and bemoans: *"There, except for ME, go I."*

Pogo Possum blurts out in the comic strip: "We have met the enemy, and *they is US!"*

Solomon said centuries ago, and all sages, philosophers and prophets agree: *As a person thinks in the heart, so is he or she.*^{Prov.23:7}

Jesus said the same thing in different words: *According to your faith, be it done unto you.*^{Mat.9:29}

Paul, emphasizing the same principle, said: *Whatever you sow, you will reap.*^{Gal.6:7}

The comedian's line, *"What you see is what you get!"* has a far deeper meaning than the suggestive analogy implies.

A. If you can envision any thing or situation or status or blessing that God offers in His Word;

B. If you carry that vision or picture or idea or concept as a seed from God;

C. If you never allow any counsel or influence or person to plant in your mind and spirit any information that contradicts that vision;

D. As sure as good seed in good ground produces a good crop, your *seed-idea* or *vision* will materialize in your life to its fullest.

You can stake your soul on that fact.

1. **When** you accept and believe in your own value, being created in God's image;

2. **When** you identify with Jesus who died to redeem you so that God in Christ can live in you;

3. **When** the information of the Bible becomes your basis for believing God's ideas about you;

4. **Then** you have the mind of Christ. [1Cor.2:16]

5. **You have** experienced what Paul explained in Ephesians 4:23; you have been *renewed in the spirit of your mind.* You think as Christ thinks.

A Gypsy family in France brought their boy to our meetings. He was born club-footed. They carried a new pair of shoes with them because they had listened to our teaching about God's Love-plan until they could *see* their son walking with normal feet, wearing normal shoes.

One night, as thousands were listening, the lad's feet became as straight and normal as mine. With tears of joy the father told the audience what had happened, and the people rejoiced as they watched the lad put on his new shoes and walk with pride for the first time in his life.

That family's *vision* was fulfilled.

A Filipino man sold his little house to buy a ticket to the city where we were teaching a great multitude of people.

He was dying of a terminal disease but he had heard about the wonderful things that were taking place, and he believed that God would restore him.

When friends urged him not to sell the house, he replied: "I'll be cured. I'll come home well, and I'll build another house. If I lie here, I will die."

He *saw* himself well again. The picture he held in his mind of God healing him was the *seed* of its own fulfillment. He was wonderfully restored and thousands of people were inspired to have faith when he told the crowd what he had done.

A family in Africa who heard about our teaching meetings, gave their chickens and a pig to the driver of a market truck so that he would allow their son to ride in the front seat for 100 miles, to the capital city, to hear our teaching and to be cured of tuberculosis.

The agreement was for one way only.

NOW I SEE A BRAND NEW ME

The son was vomiting blood and was too weak to stand. He carried a bucket to vomit into, and a rag to wipe his face.

The parents told the driver: "Our son will die in a few days. Take him there where he can hear the teaching. We hear that the God which the white man tells about is *good*. He will cure our son. Then he can walk home."

They could *picture* their son returning home, strong and well. Their dream came to pass!

The man was laid under a tree where he could hear the teaching via the loudspeakers, and he remained there for three days and nights. Villagers noticed him and brought fruit for him to eat.

The third night, Jesus Christ came to him as we were teaching, and He healed him. He came running through the crowd, pounding his chest, crying out in tears of joy that he was healed.

The faith of those parents and the vision they held in their hearts was accomplished by God Who is full of compassion and mercy to *all* who believe on Him and who call upon Him.

Your imagination is a great aid to the release of your faith-power when it is based on God's promises in His Love-plan.

Through the knowledge you are gaining, you are seeing the promise of a new miracle—a new "You", reborn through Christ. Now you will see new goals, new targets and new purposes for your life. You can never hit a target that you cannot *see*.

Now you have your model to inspire you. His name is Jesus Christ. He assumed the punishment for all of your sins and paid the price to redeem you so perfectly to God that now He can live in you just as He lived in Christ.

That is why I titled this section: *Review The New "You."*

Jesus said, *Except you are born again, you cannot see the kingdom of God.*[Jn.3:3] One needs to experience the new birth in order to *see* God at work in a human person.

Perhaps you never considered yourself as the domain of God from where He reigns, saves, blesses, restores and prospers people.

Maybe you thought He does all of those fine things from heaven.

The essence of the Christian message is the wonder of *Christ in you.*[Col.1:27] It is the miracle of *the Kingdom of God within you.*[Lu.17:21]

When you receive Him, a new "you" is born.

If anyone receives Christ, that person is a new creature; old things are passed away; all things become new.[2Cor.5:17]

You can then say like Paul, *I myself no longer live, but* **Christ lives in me.** *And the real life I now have*

NOW I SEE A BRAND NEW ME

within this body is the result of my trusting in God's Son, who loved me and gave Himself for me.^{Gal.2:20LB}

When you receive Christ by faith into your life, His Kingdom is then headquartered *in you*—which was His original plan.

Being reborn, you can *see* the kingdom of God at work in the new "You."

> You will never again *negate, reduce* or *impoverish* yourself.
>
> You will never again *condemn* what God paid so much to redeem.
>
> You will never again *put down* what God paid so much to lift up.
>
> You will never again accuse or judge what God paid so much to forgive and to make righteous.
>
> You will never again do anything to *harm* or *deteriorate* or *destroy* what God paid so much to heal, to restore and to save.
>
> You will never again *depreciate, discredit* or *disparage* what God paid so much to dignify and to make royal.
>
> You will never again *criticize* or *revile* what God esteems to be of such infinite value.

When you believe on Jesus *in you,* then you can see the real life that God created you for.

THE BEST OF LIFE

Memorize and repeat these lines the Lord inspired me to write for you:

> The me I see is Christ in me!
> Now I can be all that I see.
> Now I'm free from the no good me;
> For now I see a brand new me!
> His embassy is now in me.
> All luxury, and discovery;
> New melody—A jubilee!
> I've found the key. So, I decree,
> That the me I see, is Christ in me!

When Christ lives in you, your new life is really His *Life* in you.

You say, Jesus:

> Here is my brain; *think* through it.
>
> Here is my face; *glow* through it.
>
> Here are my hands; *touch* with them.
>
> Here are my eyes; *see* through them.
>
> Here are my ears; *listen* with them.
>
> Here are my lips; *speak* through them.
>
> Here is my heart; *love* through it.

It is vital to learn to practice the awareness of *Jesus alive in you.*

Some beautiful verses in the Bible go like this:

*Have your delight in the Almighty and **lift up your face** to God. You will pray to Him and He will hear you... When people are **cast down**, then you shall say, **there is lifting up**, and God shall save.* Job.22:26-27,29

NOW I SEE A BRAND NEW ME

What a picture of you with God at work in you! *"There is lifting up power!"* when Jesus Christ is in your life.

Lift up the hands which hang down, and the feeble knees, and make straight paths for your feet.^{Heb.12:12-13}

With Christ in you, there is no more hanging down of hands, no more feeble knees. Nothing can stay the same in you when you practice the awareness of Jesus in you!

From today, you can begin to say:

I am *somebody*! God and I are partners! We share the same *Life*! Nothing is too good for us! Nothing can stop our success! We have *lift-up power*! We are *conquerors*! We are *royal* and we are *rich*!

Say "Yes!" to what you *see* that you want to *be*!

Say "Yes!" to your greatest vision.

See yourself *being* what you want to be, *doing* what you want to do and *having* what you want to have.

See yourself *sharing* the Jesus-life, *forgiven, clean, righteous, transformed and justified.*

See yourself *healed, restored, strong, robust, resilient and energetic.*

See yourself *happy, charming, at ease, fulfilled and productive.*

THE BEST OF LIFE

See yourself *prosperous, successful, wealthy, vigorous and fortunate.*

See God in you! He is Master! See His Kingdom within you! Then resolve that you will experience God's BEST in life.

NOW I AM READY to reveal to you the sixth secret to help you get the BEST out of life. It will lift you out of the spectator-gallery and put you into the arena where you can make your life really count for yourself and for others.

60 SECOND SECRET
DAY SIX

I SEE MYSELF in God's image, redeemed by His Love and restored to Him as He created me to be.

I believe God is alive and at work in me. I act on that premise and I release His power in me. The *seed* of His faith is in me. He fulfills His dream through me.

I resist, as I would a demon, any idea that I am limited, or inferior. I reject every thought or influence that discredits my vision of the new me. Pessimism only breeds disease, failure and misery.

I will allow no one to program my life, categorize my value or rate my potential.

God, at work and alive in me, lifts me to the level of *super living*. Nothing is impossible for *Him in me.*

My house is His domain. He gives me dignity and self-esteem.

No creed, religion or person can control my vision of the new me. I see me like He sees me with His BEST in me.

THE BEST OF LIFE

SECTION SEVEN

THE PRINCIPLE OF ACTION

THE PROOF OF YOUR FAITH

SECTION 7

Part 1 — The Great Awakener of Excellence	227
Part 2 — Acting on the "Yes!" in Life	234
Part 3 — Releasing God's Creative Power	240
Part 4 — Start — and You Will Go Places	246
Part 5 — Expand — S-t-r-e-t-c-h Yourself	250
Part 6 — Energized with Enthusiasm	256
Part 7 — Life Is a Glory — Not a Grind	260
60 Second Secret — Day Seven	265

SECTION 7—Part I

The Great Awakener of Excellence

ACTION IS THE PROOF that you believe what you say. It turns on exhilaration in life.

Action frees you from the doldrums of idleness and gets you off the loafer's bench. It blocks senility and stifles cynicism.

Action takes you out of the gallery of spectators. It invigorates, energizes and vitalizes you.

Action is the exciting road to accomplishment, the key to success, the doorway to excellence and the seed of achievement.

Action transforms dreams into reality and upgrades your living standard.

Action thrusts you out ahead of the crowd, gives you respect and prestige, increases your self-esteem, makes you happy and cures loneliness, boredom and mediocrity.

Action depends on knowledge and trust—trust in *yourself*, in your *ideas*, in *other people* and in *God*.

Action turns knowledge and trust into power and achievement.

> ### SECRET NUMBER SEVEN
>
> RECOGNIZE THAT life's BEST is *plentiful* and *available to you* when you put your new knowledge about *yourself and God* into *action*. Real believing is always proven by decisive *action*. The process of achieving faith is 1) *Knowing*, 2) *Analyzing*, 3) *Choosing*, 4) *Deciding*—then the climax of that faith is 5) *Action—claiming God's BEST* because you know it belongs to you.
>
> The greatest secret to the success of our world ministry has been *action*. *We act because we believe*.

From our youth, we were taught:

A. To *believe in God*;

B. That the *Bible is true*;

C. That *Jesus is the way to God*;

D. That *He loves and wants to help everybody*;

E. That *each human being is infinitely valuable*;

F. That if people are informed about God's Love and power, *they will believe on Him and become happy, healthy, successful and productive citizens.*

THE GREAT AWAKENER OF EXCELLENCE

As young people, we made the decision that the greatest fulfillment we could enjoy in life would be to help other people achieve these goals.

Action puts us on the road to reach, touch, lift, heal, help and save hurting, lonely people all over the world.

Action thrust us out among earth's millions where our faith can be of practical value to needy people.

Action saves us from being holy sermonizers and makes us life-energizers for millions of neglected people — in nearly ninety nations already.

Action motivates us to teach only the truths that can be demonstrated in everyday human lives.

Action keeps us from being pious theoreticians; it thrusts us into public involvement where we continually put our theories to the test by lifting human persons from mediocrity to excellence.

Jesus Christ is the living example of *Action*. When you recognize HIM at work IN YOU, nothing can stop you from succeeding in life as you follow His example, proving your faith by your corresponding actions.

Jesus was an *Action*-person, an *Action*-teacher. He said: *Everyone who hears my words, and **does** them, is a **wise** person who builds his or her house upon a rock; the rains descend, the floods come, the winds* blow, and beat upon that house; and it does not fall; for it is founded upon the rock.^{Mat.7:24-27}

Obviously, the "rock" is **doing** *what the word of God says.*

If one **hears** but fails to **act accordingly**, his or her whole structure falls apart.

James used strong words when he wrote about this subject. He said: *Be a **doer** of the word and not a **hearer** only, deluding your own self.*^{Jas.1:22}

Knowledge is not enough. To transform that knowledge into **p-o-w-e-r**, *act* on what you know, *walk* in it, *practice* it, put it to the *test*, *prove* it and *build* on it.

That is what I have been privileged to experience already in nearly ninety nations during almost six decades.

I am constantly proving that these principles work. I put them to the ultimate test in human-life experiences worldwide.

These principles *lift* the fallen, *give hope* to the despondent, bring *miraculous health* to the incurable, *sight* to the blind, *success* to the desolate, *esteem* to the fallen, *dignity* to the guilty, *happiness* to the hopeless, *prosperity* to the struggling, *vitality* to the weak, *friendship* to the outcast, *courage* to the fearful, *hearing* to the deaf, *enthusiasm* to the listless, *beauty* to the undignified and *Life* to the dying.

THE GREAT AWAKENER OF EXCELLENCE

It all happens when, after we teach these life-principles, we succeed in getting people to put them into everyday practice.

That is the *Action* principle.

*Faith without deeds is **barren**.* Another translator says, *Faith without corresponding actions is **a lifeless thing**.*^{Jas.2:20}

The one who only listens in order to store knowledge, is not the producer of results.

Jesus talked about our *Big Connection* with Him in these words:

I am the vine; ***you*** *are the branches. If you abide* ***in me*** *and* ***I in you***, *you will bear much fruit.*^{Jn.15:5-8} Only the *doer* produces the fruit of God's BEST in life.

John applied this vital *Action* principle when he taught about **Love**: *Do not love in **word**, neither with your **tongue**, but love in **deed** and in **truth**.*^{1Jn.3:18}

What is the secret to dynamic *A-c-t-i-o-n*? God is alive and at work inside you.

*It is God Who is at work **in you** causing you to be **willing** and to **do** His good pleasure.*^{Phil.2:13}

God is able to do more than you can ask or think, according to His power that works in you.^{Eph.3:20}

When you absorb these powerful principles and put them into *A-c-t-i-o-n*, you release the ability of God at work within you to *do* more than you can imagine.

Acting on biblical truths means God is acting through you.

*Lo, I am **with you** always.*^{Mat.28:20} His ability is your ability. When you *do* His Word, it is *He* who actually does the creative action. *Greater is He that is **in you** than he that is in the world.*^{1Jn.4:4} You are energized by God's mighty Spirit at work within you. *You labor together **with Him**.*^{2Cor.6:1} He is the great awakener of excellence in you.

Jesus takes *nobodies* and transforms them into *somebodies*. When you *know* that He has entered your life and has recreated you by His excellence, you act with *dignity* — like *royalty* — like a "somebody."

God in you opens the door to life's BEST. He is the person-maker. He takes demoralized people and gives them new ambitions, new desires and new dreams. He imparts health to the sick and strength to the weak.

He always goes ahead of you. He leads the way. He says, *Follow me and I will **make** you...*^{Mat.4:19}

Believe Him enough to *trust* Him. Commit yourself to Him and to His *Life*style, resolving to experience His BEST.

Count on the power of Christ at work in and through you. March with a strong forward-step.

Pull yourself up from the quicksand of self-pity. Reject all negative ideas, influences, counsel and

THE GREAT AWAKENER OF EXCELLENCE

pressure. Say: *I can do all things through Christ who strengthens me.*^{Phil.4:13}

How do you do that? **Looking unto Jesus** *the author and finisher of your faith.*^{Heb.12:2} Always see Him in action *through you.*

As the art instructor said: Keep your eyes on the model; don't watch your hands.

With God, nothing will be impossible.^{Lu.1:37} *All things are possible to you when you believe.*^{Mk.9:23}

SECTION 7—PART 2

Acting on the "Yes!" in Life

BELIEVING IS ACTION. One does not really believe something until one *acts* on that premise. *All things are possible* when you *act* with the knowledge that *God is at work in you.*

Knowledge only becomes power when you *act* upon it.

Many people who can quote sacred scriptures or the philosophers, often contradict all they have memorized by their actions and their conversations.

The poverty of their language, their empty ideals and their limited outlook on life demonstrate that they are plagued by commonness, that they grope in mediocrity and that they live unstable, selfish lives. They are afraid, insecure and without purpose for the good of others.

Knowledge is meaningless until enthusiastic commitment and decisive *Action* transforms that

ACTING ON THE "YES!" IN LIFE

knowledge into *power* for the good of yourself, of your loved ones and of your community.

The most natural thing in the world is to *act* on what you believe in. You buy an airplane ticket and commit your life to that airline company when you board the plane, without examining its equipment or its performance record. You prove your *faith* by your *action*.

You put your money in the bank—money that you worked hard to save, without examining the bank personnel's credentials, and usually without verifying the bank's success record.

You trust your lawyer, butcher, grocer—and what about your physician? Or your insurance company?

You *act* positively because you *believe* in these institutions and people. You live a "Yes!" in life. You can get nowhere living a "No!"

"No!" is restricting, diminishing and demoralizing. "Yes!" is invigorating, inspiring and uplifting. Act on the *"Yes!"* in life.

Just be sure that the "Yes!" is based on God's Love-plan for you, then trust Him Who is at work in you.

Some people wonder if they can trust a power that is invisible, but the greatest powers are invisible. *Love* and *joy* cannot be seen or measured, yet they are powers that produce some of life's

THE BEST OF LIFE

BEST treasures in the form of happiness, peace and contentment.

The *sounds* of a radio and the *images* transmitted to your television screen are invisible to your sight out in the open air. Yet the lives of millions are regulated by them.

Electricity is not something that you can go out and touch in midair and analyze. Yet it keeps society functioning.

Law is invisible, untouchable. Yet you are governed by it.

The north and south poles and their magnetic fields are neither visible nor touchable. Yet every airplane that flies and every ship on the high seas is dependent upon the power they emit.

All of these powers have existed since the creation of this world. They were there all the time, provided by God for all people. But these powers had to wait until human persons began to:

1) Have *thoughts* about them;

2) *Seek proof* of their existence;

3) Conceive *dreams* of how to use them;

4) Develop *designs* for appropriating them;

5) Perfect *plans* to harness them;

6) *Commit action* to utilize them.

ACTING ON THE "YES!" IN LIFE

In that same way, our heavenly Father has created every provision, tangible and intangible, for total happiness, health, success, fulfillment and peace in life.

Those provisions are real. They exist in God's domain. They are God's Will for you. They have always been available to you. They constitute your habitat, your estate. They were created and provided for you.

But they must *wait*...

Until you entertain thoughts about God's power at work in you, producing super living;

Until you start looking in the Bible, and elsewhere for proof that these good things can materialize in your life;

Until you begin to dream about how your life can be affected by God's abundance;

Until you conceive the design of a better lifestyle for you;

Until you focus on plans to possess this *good life*;

Until you commit yourself to live in happiness, wealth, success and achievement, relying upon God at work *in you*.

You are destined for success, created for achievement, and chosen for these truths. You are being reborn into a new life.

The secrets have existed for millenniums. But they have had to *wait* for people to develop, to open their mind, to dream, to plan, to decide and to *act*.

Traditional religion has created such obstructive and paralyzing mental attitudes that many people needlessly live out their lives in mediocrity and poverty, because they have been programmed to believe that they might fall from God's grace if they become successful or wealthy.

They will tolerate sickness and physical misery, believing that these are expressions of God's loving care or of His chastisement—never knowing which, but welcoming either in a perverted form of pious resignation.

They will accept problems, defeat, or failure, without resistance or objection, believing that in this way they are pleasing God and proving their humility and resignation to His will.

Only religion could persuade people with such bizarre logistics. (I said "religion," not the real Christ-life).

God *in you* is as rich, powerful, abundant and dynamic as He was before He came to live *in you*. He did not change when He entered your life.

Jesus did not reduce Himself to your level; He exalted you to His level. You have been made an *heir of God, a joint-heir with Jesus Christ.* [Rom.8:17; Gal.4:7]

ACTING ON THE "YES!" IN LIFE

Be aware of your identification with Him. He is alive in you. All of the provisions of God's BEST in your life are available now. But they must *wait* in their invisible form until you recognize, accept and *act* upon them.

Reject any dogmas, counsel, religious creed or influence that tries to desensitize your ambition for life's BEST.

Never allow society or religion to pour you into the mold that they decide befits you. If they can indoctrinate you in the image they choose for you, and if you live as you think they think you should live, then you become their slave. You belong to them when you allow others to regulate life for you.

Never allow society, tradition or peer pressure to stalemate or to limit your finest development.

Jesus expects us to keep learning. He told us to make *disciples*. A disciple is a *learner*. I am a *learner*.

Jesus is limitless. He never stops revealing Himself. I will never stop learning about Him.

Civilization has barely touched the edge of scientific discovery. The super-abundance which God has created here tells me that there are innumerable wonders that we can continue discovering about *Him* — if we do not become indoctrinated or absolute, and stop thinking.

SECTION 7—PART 3

Releasing God's Creative Power

A SINGLE DROP OF DEW on a fresh rose petal was microscopically photographed for a television special.

Inside that tiny globe of moisture was an entire world. Infinitesimal creatures could actually be seen mating, eating, moving in organized patterns —all in a drop of fresh dew on a rose. Female species were actually photographed in the act of giving birth. That tiny drop of dew was, in itself, a microcosmic universe of life.

The depths of the seas or the mountains, the infinity of the universe—or of life in a tiny drop of dew, has not even begun to be comprehended.

Yet traditional religious teachers would have us believe that God has fully revealed everything there is to know about Himself and that we are to bow to antiquated dogmas and relegate God to primitive pontifical pronouncements.

RELEASING GOD'S CREATIVE POWER

Once a religious doctrine is approved and a position is adopted by an ecclesiastical council, it becomes a criterion for indoctrination and, once people accept it, their minds are regimented and fixed; and they stop thinking.

God has a fascinating new world for you to discover, as long as you do not allow your brain to be harnessed and regimented by others—as long as you are willing to entertain a new concept, to have a new dream, to reach for a new horizon.

You are not here to be stalemated or stagnated. You are here to become God's BEST! *All things whatsoever **you desire**, when you pray, **believe** that you receive them and you will have them.*^{Mk.11:24}

All things that you desire already exist in abundance. Otherwise, you could not receive them. They are just *waiting* for you to *act* upon the desires that you have for them. When you do, God will materialize them in your life.

All inventions are simply the result of someone's dream, plan and *action* on the basis of a provision which God had already made and that already existed.

Faith is *seeing the unseeable* and acting upon it as though it already existed in tangible form.

*We **call** those **things** which be not as though they were.*^{Rom.4:17}

THE BEST OF LIFE

We *look not at the* **things** *which* **are seen,** *but at the* **things** *which are* **not** *seen.*^{2Cor.4:18}

Things *which are* **seen** *were not made of* **things** *which* **appear**^{Heb.11:3} — or we could say, "What we *see* was made of *things* that we *cannot see.*"

This means that the *unseen* world is more real than the *seen* world, because *seen* things were all made of *unseen* things which existed in God's *unseen* domain before He materialized them in our *seen* world.

Every *thing* that you desire already exists in God's domain. It is only waiting for you to know about it and to believe it, then to transform that *knowledge* and *faith* into power by a-c-t-i-o-n.

The power which created the world cannot be *seen*. **The Best Of Life** already exists for *you* in God's realm where it awaits your recognition by faith and your *Action* to experience the *things* that you desire.

Faith is the **substance** *of* **things** *hoped for, the evidence of* **things** *not seen.*^{Heb.11:1}

What do you *hope* for? What do you want?

Do you dare to want life's BEST? Has your religion stifled your desire, clouded your dream or benumbed your aspirations?

Would you like to have — Good health? More love? Success in business? A better job? A good career? Freedom from debt? Health? Happiness?

Achievement? Freedom from fear? More self-respect? Self-dignity? Self- esteem?

All of this already exists in God's realm for you. It has your name on it. It belongs to you.

Do not permit antiquated indoctrination to block your reach for these *good* things in life.

God *is* everything *good* that you can desire.

He created this world of wealth, in tangible form and in abundance—and for you.

The fact that He transformed so much of the *unseen* world into tangible, touchable *things* that we can see and feel and experience, is proof that He wants us to enjoy those *things*.

What **things** *soever you desire,* [Jesus said]...*you will have them.*^{Mk.11:24}

Seek first the Kingdom of God...and all these **things** *will be added unto you.*^{Mat.6:33}

Your Father gives good **things** *to them that ask Him.* ^{Mat.7:11}

All **things** *are yours.*^{1Cor.3:21}

We can know the **things** *that are freely given to us of God.*^{1Cor.2:12}

His divine power has given unto us all **things** *that pertain unto life.*^{2Pe.1:3}

No good **thing** *will God withhold from them that walk uprightly.*^{Psa.84:11}

THE BEST OF LIFE

*They that seek the Lord will not want any good **thing**.*
Psa.34:10

*Your Father knows what **things** you have need of.*
Mat.6:8

Make a list of the *things* that you hope to receive, to own and to do. Believe in God's Love-plan and trust His promises enough to *act* on them, depending on God at work within you.

When you trust God's dream for you enough to put *actions* with your believing, that releases God's creative power.

All of the *things* which you have been picturing in your mind and spirit begin to materialize, just as a grain of wheat germinates, grows and produces after its kind.

1) Your *self-value*,

2) Your *identity* with Christ,

3) Your *desire* for good things,

4) Your *choice* and *decision* power,

5) Your *knowledge* of your Father's wealth,

6) Your *vision* of the new "You,"

7) And your **Action** that corresponds to this knowledge and faith releases the same creative power of God as was released when He created the world, opened the Red Sea, provided manna from heaven, or water from a rock.

RELEASING GOD'S CREATIVE POWER

Your faith in *action* releases the same power that was released when Jesus healed the cripples, restored the blind and deaf, fed the multitude and raised the dead—or when Peter and John lifted a cripple to his feet, or when Paul raised a dead man or told a lame man to walk.

SECTION 7—PART 4

Start—and You Will Go Places

WHEN YOU DECIDE to pursue life's BEST, Jesus said, *Lo, I am with you.*^{Mat.18:20} He is *in* you.

Fix your dream so clearly in your mind and spirit that you can *see* it. Write it—plainly, on cards to place on your mirrors, in your car, your wallet, on your desk, at your work bench, in your lunch container, in your kitchen and wherever you can see it and think and dream about it.

Refuse any influence or counsel, suggestion or idea that contradicts what you have decided to pursue and experience.

In Matthew 14:28-33, Peter saw the Lord walking on the water and was so inspired that he wanted to do it. And *Peter...walked on the water!*

Then the wind blew and Peter quit looking at Christ and began looking at the circumstances. He began to sink.

START—AND YOU WILL GO PLACES

But when he looked back at Jesus and cried out for help, Jesus lifted him from his sinking dilemma.

That is what He will do for *you*.

In Mark 2, A crippled man was carried to Jesus. The house where Jesus was teaching was so jammed, they could not get near the door.

They believed in Jesus' power to heal him and they *acted* accordingly.

They tore the tile from the roof and proceeded to lower the man, on his bed, with ropes and placed him before Jesus. The Bible says, *Jesus saw their faith.*$^{Mk.2:5}$ He *saw* their faith in their *actions*.

The result: Jesus forgave the man his sins and told him to *arise, to take up his bed and to go his way.* $^{Mk.5:11}$

The man did not hesitate because of his paralysis, but he *did* what Jesus said to do, and his a-c-t-i-o-n released the creative power of God to materialize his miracle. He was made whole.

They brought a man to Jesus who had a withered hand. Jesus told him to *"Stand up."* Then He said, *"S-t-r-e-t-c-h* forth your hand." In other words, *Do* something!

The man put forth all of his energy to do as Christ had commanded and his hand was restored.

THE BEST OF LIFE

In practically all of Christ's miracles, there is the clear lesson that one must *act* — must *do* something in order to obtain what one desires.

It may seem impossible, but do it anyway because God is at work within you. Your *action* by faith releases God's creative power within you for the impossible.

*The things which are IMpossible for **you** are possible for **God**.* Lu.18:27

For with God nothing will be impossible. Lu.1:37

A man was carried to our meeting who had been shot through his spine. For 16 years his legs were useless, fixed in a squatted position and withered to little more than skin and bones.

All of those years he moved about by bearing his weight on his hands and swinging his body and boney, drawn legs between them.

When he listened to the principles we were proclaiming to the public, he was transformed in his attitude about God and about himself. He discovered his own *self-value* as a creation of God.

He discovered that he could actually have God's BEST — which for him was the restoration of his legs.

He welcomed God into his life and became so happy and convinced that Christ was at work *in* Him that after prayer, he put *action* to his believing.

START—AND YOU WILL GO PLACES

With the help of a friend, he pulled himself up and, wonder of wonders, new feeling rushed into his legs, they straightened out to their full length, and he stood upright for the first time since his spine had been shattered by the bullet.

The man walked and ran, showing the huge crowd his miracle.

Being a soldier, his case is well known, a matter of government record. He has traveled and has spoken in churches, schools and public auditoriums, sharing with people the wonder of his miracle.

Action transformed his *faith* into *power*.

Heaven is never reached by the person who does not *act*. You honor truth by putting it to work for you.

The songwriter underscored this principle in this verse:

> A bell is not a bell 'til you *ring it*.
> A song is not a song 'til you *sing it*.
> Love in your heart is not put there to stay,
> Love is not love 'til you *give it away*.

The idea is always—***action!***

I say:

> *Listen* and you will hear—and be heard.
> *Look* and you will see—and be seen.
> *Reach out* and you will touch—and be touched.
> *Search* and you will discover—and be discovered.
> *Start* and you will go places.

SECTION 7—PART 5

Expand—S-t-r-e-t-c-h Yourself

JESUS WAS ALWAYS an *action*-person. Most teachers *explain* things. Jesus *did* things.

- He could have given discourses about the honor of dedicated labor.

    Instead, He just worked in a carpenter's shop.

- He could have explained theories about temptation.

    Instead, He went into the desert, confronted the tempter and conquered him.

- He could have detailed the philosophy of happiness.

    Instead, He attended weddings, banquets, parties and shared happiness with people.

- He could have talked endlessly about the infinite life of a soul.

    Instead, He just raised the dead.

EXPAND—S-T-R-E-T-C-H YOURSELF

- He could have taught entire seminars on the value and importance of children.

  Instead, He just took them up in His arms, loved them and blessed them.

- He could have lectured about the urgency for people to lift each other and to support one another.

  Instead, He just went and helped people and transformed their lives.

- He could have given valuable lessons about the equality and worth of womanhood.

  Instead, He treated women like he treated men. He healed them, blessed them, shared Life with them and even commissioned them to propagate His message. He forgave a woman taken in adultery and restored her dignity. He drove the demons out of a lady and transformed her into the first messenger of the resurrection.

- He could have taught weighty lessons on the equality of human persons.

  Instead, He just treated everybody the same. He wept when a friend died. He regarded the lowest the same as the highest. He washed His followers' feet and dried them with a towel. He gave the same attention to beggars and lepers as He did to priests and dignitaries.

- He could have lectured on the fact that spiritual things are more real than material things.

Instead, He just went out and walked on the water, multiplied bread and went through locked doors.

- He could have preached a long, accusing sermon about the sins of the crippled man and explained how his sickness was his punishment.

    Instead, He just forgave the man and told him to *rise up and walk again.*

- He could have lectured endlessly on the need for people to forgive one another.

    Instead, even when He was being spat upon, mocked and killed, He prayed for those who drove the spikes in His hands and feet and for those who thrust the spear in His side, *"Father, forgive them."*

- He could have announced profound theories about God.

    Instead, He just said, "Follow me!" "I am the way!" "If you have seen me, you have seen the Father."

Jesus was not a man of theory nor a promoter of religious doctrine. He was not a philosopher. He was a man of ***action.***

One translation says, *God is the **energizer** within you.*[Phil.2:13] *The same God does all the **energizing**.*[1Cor. 12:6]

With God at work *in* you, you are *energized* by His life.

EXPAND—S-T-R-E-T-C-H YOURSELF

God *empowers* you with strength by His Spirit. Eph.3:16

As long as you treat this knowledge as a philosophy or a theory, and wistfully dream about what it may mean to you—*someday,* His power will not be manifested in your life.

Now is the accepted time, **Now** *is the day of salvation.* 2Cor.6:2

Now is when you are what God says you are. See yourself as God's partner *now*.

Now, you have infinite *value*. You are *identified* with Christ. You are connected with abundance. All of God's *good* things are yours.

Now, is when all of these secrets are true. God is in action in you now. Salvation is yours now. God's health and wealth are yours now. You are a new person, with new power now.

Now, your life is different, changed, transformed. You are a new "You." The miracle-Jesus lives at your house *now*.

Expand—*s-t-r-e-t-c-h* yourself. Believe! Then *put action to your faith* and release the power that produces God's BEST in your life—*now*.

Theodore Roosevelt said:

> "The credit goes to the person who is actually in the arena—whose face is smeared with sweat and dirt and blood—who at his or her *best* knows in the end the triumph of high

achievement, and who at his or her *worst* at least failed while daring greatly — so that his or her name would never be among those cold and timid souls who know neither defeat nor victory."

D.L. Moody said:

"I like the way *I am doing things* more than the way you are talking about them!"

The *doer* is far superior to the *critic*, and the one who *strives* stands far above the one who *surrenders*.

I call this principle: "Action TNT." Action — Today, Not Tomorrow.

The winning crowd does not *wait* on things to happen, or *wonder* at things that happens. They *make* things happen. They do it by *action*.

God cannot *act* until *you act*. The ball is in your court. The next move is yours. No one else is responsible. Not your parents, your boss nor your community.

The apathetic and the coward laments each failure with lazy submission, moaning: "That's the way the ball bounces!" Or, "That's the way the cookie crumbles!"

But the believer *takes charge!* The *action*-person says, "I'll bounce my own ball!" Or, "I'll navigate my own vessel!" The believer makes things happen! He or she changes things!

EXPAND—S-T-R-E-T-C-H YOURSELF

Pine caterpillars have been placed end-to-end in a circle, with food in the center. They will follow each other until they die of starvation, with plenty of food within smelling distance.

The greatest waste is to permit one's life to be spent under the influence, domination or leadership of someone who is negative.

Associate with *big* people. They influence you to think *big*. Little people make you feel and think little. They retard your progress and destroy your self-esteem.

The only person who restricts your progress or obstructs your happiness, health, success and prosperity is the one who negatively influences your decisions.

Life is up to *you*—no one else.

A chain's strength is not measured by its strongest link but is limited by its weakest link.

The world is full of capable people with the talent and gifts needed to go to the top in life. But they live at the bottom because they lack the will to take inventory and to act decisively.

Someone said it is not the size of the dog in the fight, but the size of the fight in the dog that determines the winner.

SECTION 7—PART 6

Energized with Enthusiasm

I HAVE REVEALED these seven secrets to life's BEST for you because my wife and I were fortunate enough, from our youth, to have observed them then to have tested them globally.

They have brought immense happiness, healthy living, material abundance, fulfillment in marriage and super success to our lives during the fifty-four years we lived and ministered together.

I am committed to giving my remaining years to continue sharing and teaching these vital secrets to as many people as I can possibly reach, in as many nations as I am privileged to minister in.

1. This book gives you faith *in God*.
2. It gives you sound reasons to have faith *in yourself* as God's offspring.
3. It shows you why you can have faith *in your life's purpose*.

Today a new beginning is being seeded in you.

ENERGIZED WITH ENTHUSIASM

Yesterday ended last night, with all of its failures, fears, loneliness, sickness and despair—or with all of its triumphs, victories and rewarding achievements.

Today is new, with new opportunities.

Do something, even if it is imperfect. That is better than doing nothing perfectly.

Be positive. Let Jesus *energize* your life. Let Him turn on the *flow* that makes you *glow*. He breathes miracle-*Life* and miracle-*power* into you.

Seeing your life in rapport with God, releases enthusiasm in you for real living. And enthusiasm is energy—it is power.

Enthusiasm derives from the words, *"en theos"* or *"in god."* With God at work *in you*, His energy is released in you and success, happiness, health and prosperity are your rich harvest.

Today, when I step off of an airplane and walk across the tarmac or pavement of some foreign airport, I am energized with enthusiasm because of the vision I see and the goals I have set. I contemplate...

- The great audiences that I will be addressing,
- The uplifting influence that my teaching will have on that country and in her people,
- The lives that will be transformed,
- The suffering and sick people who will be healed,

- The failures in life who will grasp new hope and reach out for new success,
- The broken homes that will be restored,
- The fearful, the insecure, the lonely and the unloved human persons who will discover their value in God's Love-plan.

All of that releases a flow of joyous, uplifting enthusiasm within me. I am powerfully energized for *action* to bless thousands.

When you contemplate the seven secrets revealed in this book, and apply them in your life, fresh enthusiasm will surge within you. New, noble purpose will be focused for your life. You will be motivated for action.

The very word *"believe"* is symbolic of a power that has no human limitations.

Believers are *power*-people, *action*-people, *enthused*-people, *energized*-people.

The supreme miracle available to you is your ability to learn and to *know*; your right to choose and to *go*. It is your power to visualize your goals as though they are already tangible; it is your privilege *to take action* and to pursue the BEST in life.

You are the custodian of all of that power right now. Anything in life that is *good* and that you *desire* is within your reach — it is available to you right now!

ENERGIZED WITH ENTHUSIASM

Things which make life worth living, the achievements, inventions, discoveries, advancement in industry, science and art have all flowed from the creative power and the commitment of people...
1. Who *believed in their value,*
2. Who *dared to desire to reach higher,*
3. Who *believed in God's wealth,*
4. Who *dreamed of a better way or of a better life,*
5. Who *decided on a goal,*
6. Who *committed themselves to action,*
7. Who *fought on against obstacles until they won.*

You are one of those winners. You know the secrets now.

Your future is like a block of pure white marble. You hold the chisel and the mallet in your hands. What comes from that block must first be vivid in your vision.

So pick up your tools and begin. Keep your eyes on the image that you *see.* Keep chiseling. Never quit. You can shape your future, starting right now, into the manifestation of your greatest dream.

The same God who created Rembrandt or Leonardo Da Vinci, created you. Those men *used* their talents. They *lifted* their paint brush or chisel day after day. They dreamed and they *acted*—at first imperfectly, but never quitting—*and they won.*

SECTION 7–PART 7

Life Is a Glory—Not a Grind

YOU HAVE THE Master Artist at work in you. He chisels with your hands. He creates through you.

God works when you work. You and He are co-workers.[1Cor.3:9] So the choice is yours. He is ready when you are.

You can either wring your hands and keep losing, or roll up your sleeves and win throughout the rest of your life.

In all labor [action] *there is* **profit,** *but* **mere talk** *leads only to want.*[Prov.14:23]

Action is the big secret. *Do* something!

Focus your finest visions.

Find a need and *decide* to do something to meet it.

Find a desire and *resolve* to do something to fill it.

Find a hurt and *determine* to do something to heal it.

LIFE IS A GLORY—NOT A GRIND

Find a problem and *purpose* to do something to solve it.

In helping others to get all of the good that they desire in life, your own life will overflow with God's BEST and you will light the way for the less fortunate to follow.

With awareness of these principles, you will never impair God's work again, or demoralize His ideals, or discredit His dream, or dishonor His plan. You will never condemn God's creation or limit His power, or accuse His redeemed. You will never put down what God uplifted, or insult His nobility, or betray His trust, or make ugly what He created beautiful, or impoverish what He enriched.

The greatest treasure that you have discovered in this book is your aroused ambitions, your *renewed* courage, your revived hopes, your new possibilities and your decision to be better, happier, healthier, richer and more fulfilled.

Now you will not only attain the *good* life for yourself, but you will uplift, inspire and encourage your world.

What you now know is a sacred trust. It lifts you. It will lift people.

Say "Yes!" to your finest dreams and live with that "Yes!" ringing in your ears. Sense the delight of the *good* lifestyle, of achievement, success, dignity, respect and health.

THE BEST OF LIFE

Make life a *glory*—not a *grind*. Put beauty, happiness, riches and color in everything you think, say and do. Let your life show *God at work in you*.

Mother Teresa had a vision to go into Calcutta's slums and give dignity to the dying. She verbalized her dream: "*Doing something beautiful for God!*"

A renowned artist was asked to make a speech at the unveiling of his marble sculpture. When the veil was withdrawn, his only words were, "*There is my speech!*"

Life with loving and creative action, based on knowledge of God's Love-plan and faith in His promises, is powerful and creative. It produces the BEST. Its harvest is tangible. That kind of life needs no eulogy in words.

1. Decide *what* you want.
2. Analyze *why* you want it.
3. Determine *when* you want it.
4. *Picture* it before you.
5. *Plan* your steps to get it.
6. *Write* your goal and repeat it.
7. Then *go for it* and *stick with it*.

My wife loved to say:

"In trying times, never stop trying!"

"In hard times, get harder!"

LIFE IS A GLORY—NOT A GRIND

"In tough times, get tougher!"

"In weak times, get stronger!"

1. Take control of your life. Be an *action*-person.
2. Never expect circumstances to be perfect.
3. Remember that knowledge, dreams and even faith are not enough. *Action* is the power-igniter.
4. If there is fear, deliberately do what frightens you, and destroy the negative power of fear.
5. Commit yourself to action, then. Go! Never wait for an emotional surge.
6. Think in terms of "*n-o-w!*" —not tomorrow, not next week, not next year.
7. Break the static grip of inaction. *Do* something. Give it all you have and life will give you all it has—and God's life has plenty.

Say to yourself:

- I have been put here to be happy and healthy, to live in abundance and to succeed in life.
- I will never apologize for my happiness, health, success or abundance.
- I will put my talents and abilities into *action* and set my self to achieve life's fullest and BEST.
- I do not have to suffer now to be worthy of happiness in heaven.

THE BEST OF LIFE

- I am full of God's Life now.
- The Master is at work in me.
- Being created in God's image and placed here on this earth is all the authority I need for success, happiness, health and prosperity.
- I am in control of my own life.
- I have the power to believe and to decide the level of life I will settle for.
- I prefer excellence to mediocrity.
- I accept full responsibility for my thoughts, decisions, goals and actions—for the results of my life.
- I will never hinder my own success, happiness, health or prosperity.
- I deserve life's BEST. I am surrounded by it. It is my rightful estate. God put it here for me and He put me here for it.
- I am talented. I have a good mind and the power to control it. God is at work in me through the abilities He has entrusted me with.
- I will not wait for the world of good things to come to me. I couple *action* with my believing. That is the proof of my faith.
- I choose life's BEST!

LIFE IS A GLORY—NOT A GRIND

60 SECOND SECRET
DAY SEVEN

ACTION IS THE PROOF of what I believe. By *action* I transform my *knowledge* into *power*, turning my *possibilities* into *realities*. All things are possible when I *act* with God at work in me.

Action produces the rich fruit of God's BEST in my life. It releases His power in me. He awakens excellence in me.

Mediocrity, failure and weakness belong to those who are afraid to *act*.

I shall never allow religion or tradition to stifle my desires, to cloud my dreams or to benumb my ambitions.

God is everything *good* that I can desire or need. When I *act*, He *acts* to materialize His BEST in my life. He is my energizer.

I am resolved to go for life's BEST.

God says "YES!" to my finest dreams.

OSBORN INTERNATIONAL
Ministry To Millions

THE MISSION of Christianity is to witness of Christ to *all the world*, to *every creature*.^{Mk.16:15} The Apostle Paul was consumed with this passion.

He said, *Whoever shall call on the name of the Lord shall be saved.*^{Rom.10:13}

Then Paul asked the pivotal questions that have motivated the Osborns in each arm of their global ministry:

How shall they call on him in whom they have not believed? and how shall they believe in him of whom they have not heard? and how shall they hear without a preacher? and how shall they preach except they be sent? ^{Rom.10:14-15}

In 1949, OSBORN INTERNATIONAL was instituted *to express and propagate the Gospel of Jesus Christ to all people throughout the world.* Their **maxim**: *No one deserves to hear the Gospel repeatedly until everyone has heard it once.* Their **motto**: *One Way – Jesus; One Job – Evangelism.* Their guiding **principle**: *Every Christian believer – a witness for Christ.*

During almost six decades, they have proclaimed the Gospel to millions in close to ninety nations.

OSBORN INTERNATIONAL MINISTRY TO MILLIONS

Dr. Daisy Osborn passed away in 1995. Dr. LaDonna, the Osborn daughter, as CEO and Vice-President of OSBORN INTERNATIONAL, is making possible the expansion of ministry in many new fields such as Russia, Afrique Francophone, Eurasia and China.

As a world evangelist, Dr. LaDonna's passion to win souls drives her to the remote corners of the earth. As a pastor, her passion to build Christians into dynamic witnesses for Christ motivates her in teaching the truths of Redemption. As Bishop of over 600 churches and ministry leaders, her passion to help pastors and evangelists to grasp God's vision energizes her in apostolic ministry both at home and abroad.

Dr. LaDonna's teaching on Redemption is establishing new believers and training Church leaders in the dynamics of Christ-centered ministry. Her newest book, GOD'S BIG PICTURE, is already published in Russian, Bulgarian, the national Chinese language of Mandarin, and in Portuguese.

Her presentation of the biblical Gospel message through books, audio and video teachings and through her life-changing Bible courses has become the hallmark of her international ministry. She says: *The world is the heart of the Church and the Church is the hope of the world,* adding, *The passion that sent Christ to the cross is the passion that sends us to the lost.*

She contends: *Without the world, the Church is meaningless, and without the Church, the world is hopeless.*

It is her resolve to faithfully proclaim the same *Gospel message* that has been heralded by her brave parents for over a half-century in nearly ninety nations of the world.

As this book goes to press, this world missionary church organization, OSFO INTERNATIONAL is approaching its sixth decade. From its inception in 1949, it has followed the example of Paul's unrelenting quest to bring the light of the Gospel to those in spiritual darkness.

T.L. and Daisy Osborn went to India as missionaries in 1945. Not knowing about miracles, they were unable to convince Moslems and Hindus about Christ. Heartbroken, they returned to the USA realizing that people must have proof of the Gospel and evidence that Jesus is alive. *Jesus of Nazareth was...**approved of God** among people by **miracles** and **wonders** and **signs**, which God did by him in the midst of the people.*[Ac.2:22]

The Lord mercifully guided them through their dilemma. Christ appeared to T.L. (and later to Daisy). Then they discovered biblical truths that build faith for miracles today.

Their ministry of World Evangelism began back in the era when so-called "Third World" nations were dominated as European colonies. In open

OSBORN INTERNATIONAL MINISTRY TO MILLIONS

air campaigns, they addressed audiences of from 20,000 to 300,000 throughout the dangerous years of nationalism and the political rejection of colonialism.

Because of the apostolic example of their ministry in action, and through their books, docu-miracle videos and tons of literature, tens of thousands of national men and women have arisen with fresh faith and have become great Gospel ministers to the unreached. Many of them are among the successful Christian leaders in nations of the world today.

OSBORN INTERNATIONAL has sponsored over thirty thousand national preachers as full time missionaries, to their own and neighboring unreached areas, and has sponsored the establishing of new churches in over a hundred thousand tribes and villages that were previously unchurched.

The OSBORN Gospel literature is published in 132 languages. OSBORN docu-miracle crusade films, audio and video cassettes, and Bible courses for study and for public evangelism, are produced in over seventy major languages.

Huge shipments of soulwinning tools for Gospel missions and for Christian workers have been airlifted and surface-shipped to nations around the world.

Scores of four-wheel drive mobile vehicles have been provided for reaching the unreached with the Gospel worldwide. Each one has been loaded with films, projectors, screens, generators, public-address systems, audio cassettes and cassette players, plus enormous quantities of literature in one hundred and thirty-two languages.

The OSBORN books have affected millions of lives. Dr. Daisy's five major books are unprecedented in Christian literature *for women,* revealing their identity, dignity, equality and destiny in God's redemptive plan.

In 1951 T.L. wrote his first book, HEALING THE SICK. It has penetrated the world and is now in its enlarged 46th edition. Over a million copies are in print. A unique 512 page documentary, THE GOSPEL ACCORDING TO T.L. & DAISY, is published as their international witness that the Christ of Bible days is unchanged today. It is *unique* – unlike any other publication that has yet been published.

Today, OSBORN INTERNATIONAL is esteemed as a preeminent voice in world missions for this 21st Century. Its programs are making a global impact upon the lives of millions of people.

When dates can be synchronized, Dr. LaDonna and her father, Dr. T.L., minister together in their *Miracle-Life Seminars, Bible Equality Events* and *Public Miracle Festivals.* They share the crusade preaching, the public mass ministry to the sick, and the seminar teaching, bringing new faith, hope, and love – and *Life* to multitudes of people worldwide.

OSBORN INTERNATIONAL MINISTRY TO MILLIONS

Dr. LaDonna Osborn has become a decisive influence in world missions. All four of her children are involved in world missions. Her eldest son, Rev. Tommy, has imitated his grandfather, Dr. T.L., conducting great Gospel crusades in over fifty nations of the world. Her son, Rev. Donald, has ministered in Romania, USA, Bolivia, Chile and is now establishing new churches in Ecuador. Both daughters, LaVona and Daneesa, minister in their home churches, and alternate in traveling with their mother, assisting her in ministry and photographing her meetings in nations abroad. Daneesa, and her husband have served as missionaries in Russia and in India.

The Osborn family is determined that the nations and the peoples of Century 21 will realize 1) that the Bible is valid today, 2) that the mission of each believer is to win the lost to Christ, 3) that every Christian is to be Christ's witness, and 4) that the supernatural is what distinguishes Christianity from the religions of the world.

These issues constitute the essence of the OSBORN INTERNATIONAL ministry. The witness of T.L., of his daughter, LaDonna, of his grandchildren and already of some of his great grand children, is expressed best by the words of John: *We bear record of the Word of God, and of the testimony of Jesus Christ, and of the things that we have seen.*[Rev.1:2] *We...testify of these things and have written them: and we know that our testimony is true.*[Jn.21:24]

GLOBAL PUBLISHER
OSBORN PUBLICATIONS
P.O. Box 10
Tulsa, OK 74102 USA

✧✧✧

FRENCH DISTRIBUTOR
ÉDITIONS
MINISTÈRES MULTILINGUES
909, Boul. Roland-Therrien
Longueuil, Québec J4J 4L3 Canada

✧✧✧

GERMAN PUBLISHER
SHALOM — VERLAG
Pachlinger Strrasse 10
D-93486 Runding, CHAM, Germany

✧✧✧

PORTUGUESE PUBLISHER
GRACA EDITORIAL
Caixa Postal 1815
Rio de Janiero–RJ–20001, Brazil

✧✧✧

SPANISH PUBLISHER
LIBROS DESAFIO, Apdo. 29724
Bogota, Colombia

(For Quantity Orders, Request Discount Prices.)